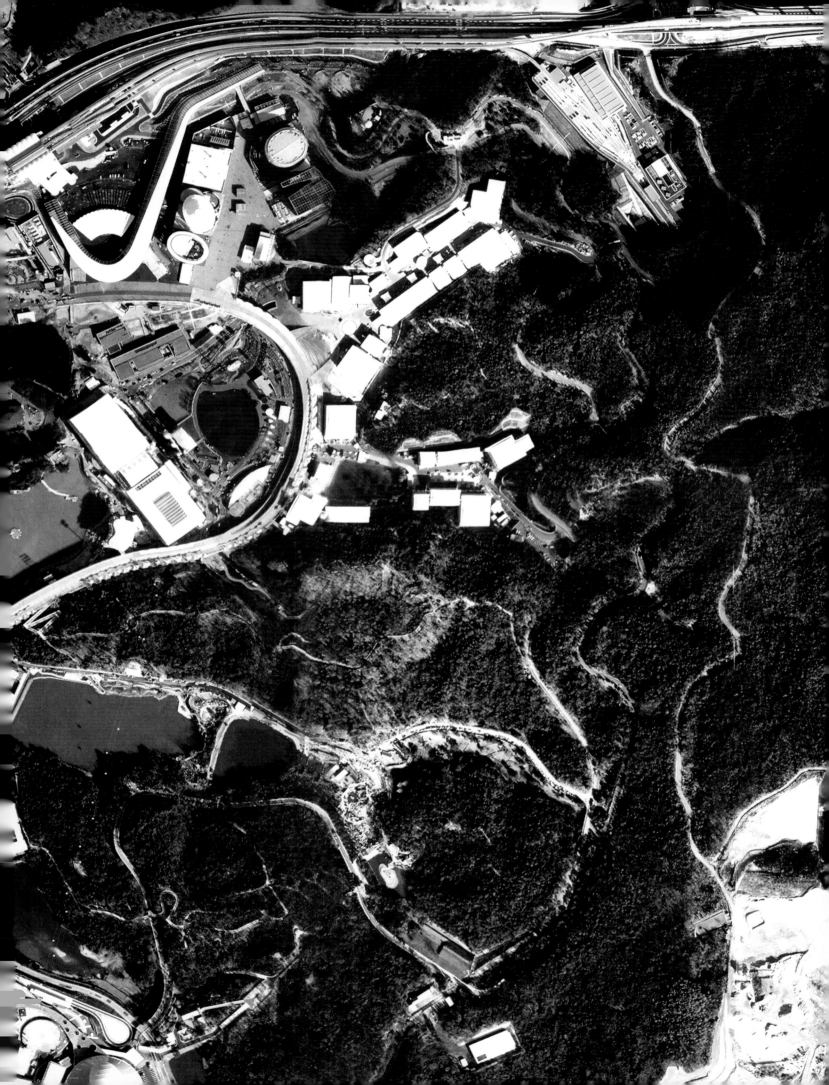

Title:2005 World Exposition Aichi Japan
Publisher:Sandu Cultural Media (HongKong) Co., Ltd
Address: Unit B, 10/F. Kolling Center, 77-79 Granville Road,
Tsim Sha Tsui, Kowloon, Hong Kong
Compiler:Sandu Cultural Media
Producer:Design Department of Sandu Cultural Media
Website:www.sandu168.com
E-mail Address:sd_168@163.net
ISBN 988-98566-1-1

Contents

Europe & Mediterranean Zone

Europe Zone

The Americas Zone

SPLENDID EXPOSITION, CHINA IN EXPECTANCY

Two of the three world expositions in the first decade of 21st century will be held in Asia, which gives expression to the increasingly important role Asia plays in international economic and political affairs. On March 25th, 2005, Expo 2005 Aichi, Japan rang up the curtain, in which intelligent robots became the highlight. The three Rs (Reduce, Reuse, Recycle) advocated by Japan have evoked worldwide repercussion among environmentalists. With the approaching of 2010, Shanghai (China) will host the next world exposition. We are expecting all the splendors. The following are the history of the World Exposition and the features of the present exposition in Aichi, Japan, through which you can obtain a much clearer view.

All Begins with the World Exposition.

Up until now, the World Exposition has been in existence for 150 years. It is an international event exerting far-reaching influence. On one hand, it makes a veritable record of the development of modern science and technology; on the other hand, it enkindles the flame of imagination and smashes shackles on thoughts.

The World Exposition originates in the regular gathering in Middle Age of European merchants --- Fair. At the very beginning, the fair functioned as an occasion for on-the-spot trading. Entering 19th century, the fair had a larger and larger scale with ever increasing influence. Around 1820s, large-scale fairs were called exhibitions whose function turned gradually into exchange of commodities and display of achievements.

Mid-19th century witnessed the prime of British industrialization. Britain became Super Power in Europe, and even in the whole world, as a result of its completion of Industrial Revolution and colonial expansion. In order to make a show of its greatness and pride, the British Empire staged a magnificent fair named Great Exhibition in Crystal Palace made of steel and glass, situated in Hyde Park, London. It feasted visitors' eyes with about 1400 precious works of art and fashion products. As an epoch-making pioneering undertaking, the London exhibition is regarded as the first World Exposition.

With the springing up of America, New York hosted the second World Exposition in 1853, which opened up a new agricultural section. In addition, a kind of escalator equipped with safety devices made its first appearance. The New York Exposition was much acclaimed.

In 1855, Paris in the reign of Louis Bonaparte put on the third World Exposition, in which concrete, plastic and aluminum products came into view. The originality lied especially in that foreign heads of state were invited to visit the site, which was the first time in its history and thus initiated a new custom in arts exhibition and which was carried on by all the following occasions. There were in total eight world expositions in the 19th century.

In the 20th century, world expositions were mainly held in developed countries such as America and some European countries. With a view to reducing the excessive frequency and cutting down fiscal expenditure, official delegates from 35 countries signed a treaty in Paris in 1928, laying down rules for the holding of world expositions, for instance that each world exposition needs to have a particular theme, and that the duration is limited within 6 months etc.

Each world exposition has unique features and introduces the latest development in science and technology, so it has become a grand meeting attracting worldwide attention. The function of the World Exposition keeps on improving and extending. Up to now, its functions range from the former technological exchange and academic discussion to tourism, sightseeing and entertainment. Its influence on life is positive and profound. As it is put in the slogan: "All begins with the World Exposition."

The World Exposition 2005, Aichi, Japan: Nature's Wisdom

With the marvelous advancement of science and technology, all the world is undergoing a dramatic change. However, human activities have brought ruinous consequences for the earth. The transformation and reduction of energy, and the destruction and pollution of eco- environment leave us a much damaged earth. The frequent tsunami, earthquake and flooding are the alarm sounded by nature.

In the 21st century, human beings need to solve the problem of sustainability world around and foster a kind of society that harmonizes humanity with nature. This world exposition in Aichi, Japan, therefore chooses "Nature's Wisdom" as its theme, with the following three sub-themes:

1. The origin of nature: The show applies the latest space-technology, the frontier of life-science development and Information technology.

2. The art of life: The show includes feelings of respecting nature, ways of harmonious living with nature and artistic achievements originated from nature.

3. The cycle-type society: The show includes the current situation and prospect forecast of the global environment, the influence of climatic change on life and environment as well as cycle utilization and protection of resources and energy.

The five concepts advocated in Aichi Expositon are:

1. Through the Global Loop various wisdom for life meeting;

2. Being moved by the wonderful earth we live on;

3. Japan's environment, science and technology on display;

4. The first exposition with citizens' participation;

5. The newest technological achievements.

Aichi World Exposition has two sites, Nagakute and Seto respectively. It is divided further into several zones, such as Global Commons, Corporate Pavilion Zone, Central Zone, Japan Zone, Interactive Fun Zone, and Forest Experience Zone etc. There are totally 6 Global Commons that draw worldwide attention.

Global Common 1: Here are mainly countries from Asia continent. The design emphasizes symmetry and the use of straight lines.

Global Common 2: Here are mainly countries from northern, middle and southern American continent, with a pool in the center and trees around.

Global Common 3: Mediterranean and European countries assemble at this area. It is situated in Global Loop, having the advantage of convenient transportation.

Global Common 4: It's an area for European, especially northern European countries. It is directly accessible by gondola from the North Gate and via IMTS (Intelligent Multi-mode Transit System) buses from the Non-Official Participation Zones.

Global Common 5: It's a zone for African countries. The Africa Pavilion is very spacious with displays from many African countries.

Global Common 6: This is a zone for countries from Oceania and Southeast Asia. The strewn-at-random design has greatly enhanced the scenery.

Japan's advanced technology is collectively displayed in the 9 pavilions in Corporate Pavilion Zone, including: Wonder Circus - Electric Power Pavilion, JR Central Pavilion, JAMA Wonder Wheel Pavilion, Mitsubishi Pavilion @Earth, Toyota Group Pavilion, Hitachi Group Pavilion, Mitsui-Toshiba Pavilion, Mountain of Dreams, and Gas Pavilion.

Through an overall introduction, and details about the Global Commons and Corporate Pavilion Zone, this book will give a full coverage and insightful interpretation of this magnificent World Exposition.

China and the World Exposition

In the 150 years' history of the World Exposition, China has been an active participant. According to historical materials, Deqiong Xu from Xangshan Guangdong took part in the first World Exposition with his own product "Rong Ji Hu Si" in 1851, winning a gold medal and a silver one awarded by Queen Victoria. From then on, China has participated for many times and won numerous medals. In the Panama World Exposition in 1915, Chinese products won totally 1211 prizes, including 258 gold medals, 337 silver medals, 258 bronze medals, and 74 honorary prizes, and 227 certificates of merit etc.

The World Exposition is beyond doubt an international gathering for exchange. Aichi has handed a satisfactory examination paper. What will become of Shanghai World Exposition? Active promotion of urbanization in China will be easily noticed from the theme of Expo 2010 Shanghai China "Better City, Better Life", and its sub-themes "Integration of divers cultures in the city; Prosperity of urban

new economy; Re-establishment of urban communities; Interaction between the city and village",
which are multiplied and diversified.

Look forward to 2010, with our sincere wishes that Shanghai will host an even more brilliant World
Exposition.

History of the World Exposition

2005 Aichi Japan: Nature's Wisdom

2000 Hanover Germany: Humankind, Nature, and Technology

1998 Lisbon Portugal: Oceans- a Heritage for the Future

1993 Taejon South Korea: A New Road Forward

1992 Seville Spain: Age of Discovery

1992 Genoa Italy: Ship and Ocean

1991 Plovdiv Bulgaria: Youth activity for a peaceful World

1988 Brisbane Australia: Leisure in the Age of Technology

1986 Vancouver Canada: Transportation and Communication

1985 Tsukuba Japan: Livings and Surroundings - Science and Technology for Man at home

1985 Plovdiv Bulgaria: Wellings and surrendings science and technology for man at home

1982 Knoxville USA: Energy Turns the World

1965 Munich Germany: IVA-International Transport Exhibition

1964 New York USA: Peace Through Understanding

1962 Seattle America: The Human Being in the Space Age

1961 Turin Italia: Centenary Celebration of the Unification of Italy

1958 Brussels Belgium: Evaluation of the World for a more human world

1957 Berlin Germany: Reconstruction of Hansa Area

1956 Israel: Citriculture

1955 Helsingborg Sweden: Art and Profession

1955 Turin Italy: Sport

1954 Naples Italy: Navigation

1951 Lille France: Textile

1949 Stockholm Sweden: Universal Sport Exhibition

1949 Port au Prince Haiti: Bicentennial of the foundation of Port-au-Prince

1939 New York USA: Building the World of Tomorrow

1939 Liege Belgium: Season of Water

1938 Helsinki Finland: Aviation and Aerospace

1937 Paris France: Arts and Techniques in Modern Life

1935 Brussels Belgium: Peace through Competitions

1933: Chicago USA: A century of Progress

1929 Barcelona Spain: Exposition International de Barcelona

1929 Philadelphia USA: Celebration of 150th Anniversary

1915 San Francisco USA: Inauguration of the Panama Canal and celebration of the construction
of San Francisco

1913 Ghent Belgium: Universal and International Exhibition

1910 Brussels Belgium: Universal and International Exhibition

1906 Milan Italy: Exposizione Internazionable del Sempione

1905 Liege Belgium: 75th Anniversary of Belgium Independence

1904 Louisiana USA: Celebration of the Centennial of the purchase of Louisiana

1900 Paris France: Evaluation of a century

1897 Brussels Belgium: Exposition International de Bruxelles

1894 Chicago USA: The Fourth Centennial of the discovery of America

1889 Paris France: Celebration of the Centennial of France Revolution 1789

1888 Barcelona Spain

1883 Amsterdam Holland

1880 Melbourne Australia: International Exhibition of arts, Manufactures and Agricultural and
Industrial Products of all Nations

1878 Paris France: Agriculture, Industry and Art

1876 Philadelphia USA: Celebration of the Centennial of American Independence

1873 Vienna Austria: Culture and Education

1867 Paris France: Agriculture, Industry and Art

1862 London Britain: Agriculture, Industry and Art

1855 Paris France: Agriculture, Industry and Art

1851 London Britain

001-014

Zone : Japan Zone

Pavilion : Japan Pavilion Nagakute

Note : The theme of NAGAKUTE NIPPON-KAN is "Experience Japan, from the affluence of the 20th century to the affluence of the 21st century - Let's grow closer to nature again".

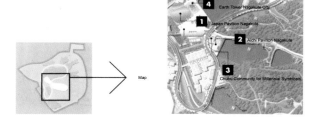

001

002

① Bamboo cage
The bamboo cage will reduce the quantity of solar energy striking the building. The cage will suppress the thermal load and, at the same time, will merge in well with the natural environment.
② Biomass construction
Wooden building made of timber from thinning.
③ Roof
Air trapped between the bamboo slats and the plywood shingles will reduce heat transmission from the outside air.
④ Walls
The effectiveness of the thermal insulation will be enhanced by biodegradable plastics that will degrade to soil and by air pockets trapped between the materials. Green walls will reduce the thermal load.

⑤ Ozone treatment system
This system will produce semi-treated water(not for drinking) from sewage.
⑥ Room made of photo-catalytic steel plates
Photo-catalytic steel plates and a sprinkling system using semi-treated produced by the ozone treatment system will enhance the effectiveness of cooling of the building.
⑦ Bundled pillars
Pillars made of bundled timber from thinning.
⑧ Space where people spend time
Only the places where people spend time will be air conditioned to reduce energy consumption.

001-006

Zone : Japan Zone

Pavilion : Japan Pavilion Nagakute

Item : The Construction

Note : The entire building is covered by a bamboo cage that acts as a thermal insulator. The pavilion is constructed using as much environmentally friendly technology as possible. All of the electricity consumed in the pavilion is generated by renewable energy. Energy consumption is cut by supplementing the air conditioning with the bamboo cage, a roof made of photo-catalytic steel plates and green walls. Plastic construction materials made from timber from thinning and plants, etc. is used for the pavilion. The entire building is a trial construction for new technologies and materials.

006

007

007

Zone : Japan Zone

Pavilion : Japan Pavilion Nagakute

Item : Earth Room

Note : The room provides you with a video simulation that shows the Earth's vitality. You will be embraced in the Earth's vitality as you enter a sphere with a diameter of 12.8m (1: 1 million scale of the Earth). It is the world's first all-sky video system covering 360 degrees. You will enjoy feeling the Earth's natural vitality and its splendor, and cherishing the sense of belonging to the Earth.

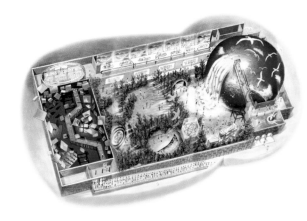

008

008-011

Zone : Japan Zone
Pavilion : Japan Pavilion Nagakute
Item : Ties between Man and Nature
Note : "Life-to-life", "man-to-man", and "technology-to-nature" relationships are three important "relationships" embodying in three spaces. You will encounter here the healing power of forests. Imagine "Nature's Wisdom", while immersing yourself in forest environment created through effective use of light, sound, scent, and image. You will get comfort and delight by feeling connected to the nature.

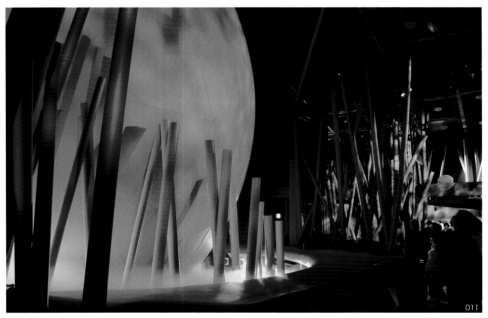

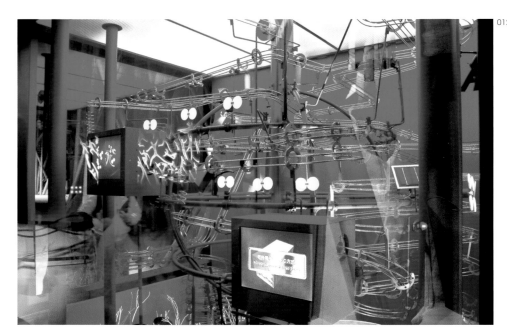

012
Zone : Japan Zone
Pavilion : Japan Pavilion Nagakute
Item : Scientific Simulation
Note : Vivid demonstration of energy and power technology via video simulation and images etc attracts curious kids and those interested in science and technology.

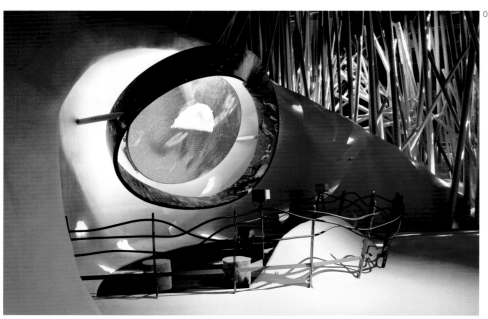

013
Zone : Japan Zone
Pavilion : Japan Pavilion Nagakute
Item : Detail of the Exhibition
Note : Centered upon "Nature and Life", the natural eco-cycling system and the source of life (DNA genetic factors) are introduced via multi media.

014
Zone : Japan Zone
Pavilion : Japan Pavilion Nagakute
Item : Detail of the Exhibition
Note : The dynamic multi-media model displays the materials, structures and new technology with which Japan Pavilion Nagakute is constructed.

001-014

Zone : Japan Zone

Pavilion : Earth Tower

Note : Visitors to this pavilion will experience the wonders of light, wind, and water. When visitors enter this approximately 40-meter-high tower ---- the world`s biggest kaleidoscope and look up from the viewing space, they will see a mysterious rising ball of light some 36 meters in diameter.

001

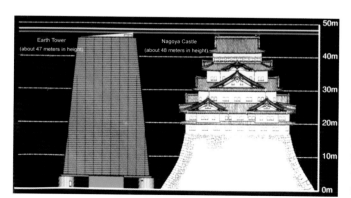

001

Zone : Japan Zone

Pavilion : Earth Tower

Item : Construction and Environment

Note : Earth Tower can be rated as the biggest kaleidoscope in the world, which is also the symbol of this region. When lighted up at dusk, it has an air of solemnity.

002

002-006

Zone : Japan Zone
Pavilion : Earth Tower
Item : Construction and Environment
Note : At the side of the lake, the imposing Earth Tower enjoys pleasant surroundings.
The striped design after the mode of fences makes the space in good order.

007

008

009

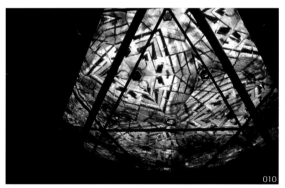

010

011

007-009

Zone : Japan Zone

Pavilion : Earth Tower

Item : Construction and Environment

Note : Around the pavilion are implements that convert the wind into sound. The exterior walls shimmer with flowing water that forms all kinds of patterns on the rocky surface. A number of lights resembling cut-paper lanterns are around the tower, approximately 2 meters in height. In the 118 lights are about 2,000 designs of various cut-paper images submitted by residents. The director in general Fumiya Fujii, eminent musician in Japan and CG artist, said that he wanted to make Earth Tower a pavilion that would draw out easiness and kindness of the human heart.

010-014

Zone : Japan Zone
Pavilion : Earth Tower
Item : Construction and Environment
Note : Earth Tower is a three-sided trapezoidal structure with a height of 47 meters. Devices installed at the top of the structure are mobile and revolve, causing spherical images approximately 40 meters in diameter, changing in shape and color, to be projected onto the inner walls.

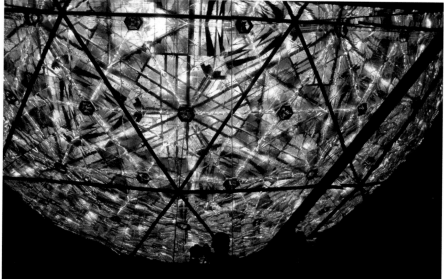

012

013

014

001-011

Zone : Japan Zone

Pavilion : Aichi Pavilion

Note : The exterior of the pavilion expresses the motif of a parade float. Its theme is "Eco-Industrial Revolution". An eco-industrial revolution is an industrial revolution that places priority on the environment, which is coined by Director of the pavilion. The pavilion also displays the traditional techniques and cutting-edge technology that are the pride of Aichi Prefecture, and promotes the new industrial structure centered on environment.

004

005

004-005

Zone : Japan Zone
Pavilion : Aichi Pavilion
Item : Moving Monument
Note : The symbolic welcome tower "Moving Monument" with "Karakuri"doll (mechanical doll) is 18 meters in height, made up of 3 iron towers and a giant lantern-shaped stage in center.

006-009

Zone : Japan Zone
Pavilion : Aichi Pavilion
Item : Details of Construction
Note : The steady wooden structure and flickering
red lanterns are very Japanese.

009

010

Environmantally Friendly Materials

011

010-011
Zone : Japan Zone
Pavilion : Aichi Pavilion
Item : Details of Construction
Note : The paper wall and its peculiar grain and property bring forth comfort and ease. It is light, ventilating and environmentally friendly.

Corporate Pavilion Zone

テーマシアター　　積水ハウス　　中部日本放送　　東

001-005

Zone : Corporate Pavilion Zone
Pavilion : JR Central Pavilion
Note : The theme of this pavilion is "Super conducting Maglev takes off!-Beyond the threshold of existing surface transit systems-." At the image theater, there is first a pre-show in front of the entrance presenting images concerning the technological development of the super conducting linear motor car and other background information. Visitors are able to experience what it is like to ride on a superconducting linear motor car via powerful three-dimensional images.

001

002

002-003

Zone : Corporate Pavilion Zone
Pavilion : JR Central Pavilion
Item : Exhibition
Note : This exhibit features a linear motor car that reached a speed of 581 kph at the Yamanashi Linear Test Line---a world speed record for a manned rail car. The car exhibited is the double-cusp MLX-01-01 invented by the company.

004-005

Zone : Corporate Pavilion Zone
Pavilion : JR Central Pavilion
Item : The Exterior

003

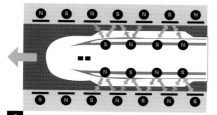

1

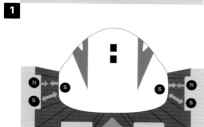

2

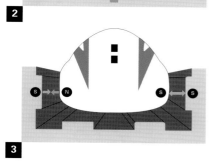

3

004

005

001-014

Zone : Corporate Pavilion Zone
Pavilion : Mitsu-Toshiba Pavilion
Note : This is a pleasantly cool pavilion covered by water. The pavilion provides entertainment that everyone can enjoy, based on the theme of "the Earth and the Radiance of Life."

001-005

Zone : Corporate Pavilion Zone
Pavilion : Mitsu-Toshiba Pavilion
Item : Architectural Features
Note : The construction adopts elements of the earth such as water, light and wind etc, displaying to the nth degree the vitality of life on earth. The outside wall of the pavilion is not closed up; instead it takes the shape of a louver covered with an "aqua wall" of running water that provides visitors with a sense of coolness and comfortableness. The Aqua Wall is formed of droplets falling into a catch drain from a height of 4.5 meters after water is pumped to the 16-meter-high roof and flows over the louver windows at the front of the pavilion. It brings a cooling breeze into the interior and limits the range of the air-conditioning to the theater in order to reduce air-conditioning load.

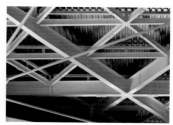

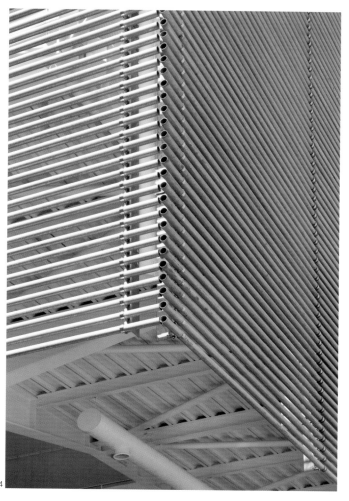

004

005

006-008

Zone : Corporate Pavilion Zone
Pavilion : Mitsu-Toshiba Pavilion
Item : Architectural Features
Note : The wall has a steel framework, which is covered by a special coarse cloth similar to white canvas, so it is light, photic and ventilating. Especially in the evening, colorful light passing through the walls, the entire building is brilliant and glittering, reminding you of its theme "the Earth and the Radiance of Life."

009-011

Zone : Corporate Pavilion Zone
Pavilion : Mitsu-Toshiba Pavilion
Item : Architectural Features
Note : The pavilion is draughty and bright. Ascending with the moving staircase, visitors are fascinated with the scenery.

009

010

011

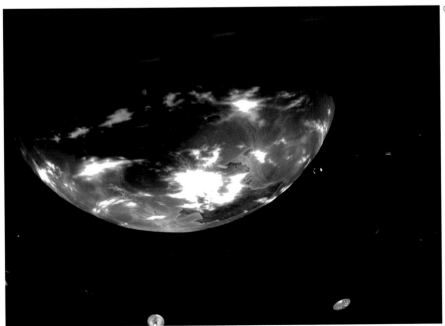

012-014
Zone : Corporate Pavilion Zone
Pavilion : Mitsu-Toshiba Pavilion
Item : "Space Child Adventure'Grand Odyssey"
Note : The main attraction is the theater in which visitors participate. The world's first "futurecast system" will instantly scan the faces of all who enter and convert them into computer graphics that will be displayed on the theater screen and be roles in the powerful space adventure titled "Space Child Adventure (Grand Odyssey)".

001-011
Zone : Corporate Pavilion Zone
Pavilion : Mitsubishi Pavilion
Note : The theme of this pavilion is: "The Wonder of Our Lives on Earth-A Glimpse of the Miracle."The outside of the pavilion presents an image of an endless, spiraling single wall. The foundation of the construction has no piles. Materials for the main structure are recyclable such as single tubes.

004-006

Zone : Corporate Pavilion Zone
Pavilion : Mitsubishi Pavilion
Item : Architectural Features
Note : Giving consideration to the environment, the outer wall is constructed of such materials as rocks, plastic bottles and plants. The green roofs and walls can not only reduce air-conditioning, but also be good for forest protection.

007-009

Zone : Corporate Pavilion Zone
Pavilion : Mitsubishi Pavilion
Item : Robot Wakamaru
Note : Visitors to the pavilion will be greeted by the robot Wakamaru, who will escort them to the exhibit "What If the Moon Didn't Exist?"

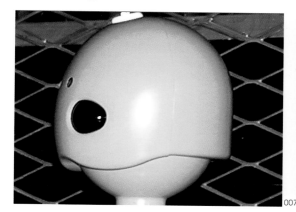

007

007

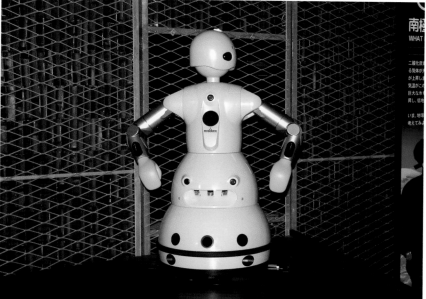

008

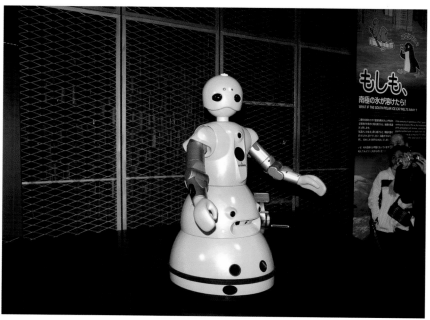

009

地球環境の維持のために共に生きる叡智を
Let us unite our wisdom for environmental preservation.

010

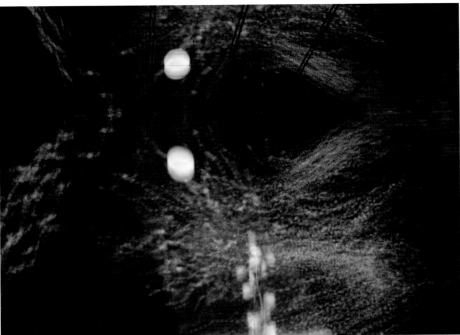

011

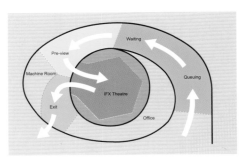

010-011

Zone : Corporate Pavilion Zone

Pavilion : Mitsubishi Pavilion

Item : "What If the Moon Didn't Exist?"

Note : This theater-style pavilion will examine what the Earth would look like if the moon did not exist, based on the book "What if the Moon Didn't Exist" by U.S. astrophysicist Neil F. Comins. A video image of a desolate Earth without the moon will be presented. After experiencing this firsthand, everyone will feel deeply that without the company of the moon, our earth will be so lonely and miserable, and thus begin to make retrospection, to cherish all the seemingly ordinary blessings of nature and to really understand the true meaning of harmony between man and nature.

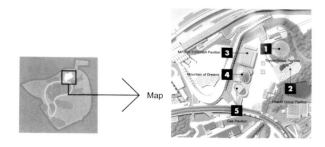

001-011

Zone : Corporate Pavilion Zone
Pavilion : Toyota Group Pavilion
Note : The pavilion adopts the theme:"The Dream, Joy and Inspiration of Mobility in the 21st Century." Through performances featuring the i-unit (a future concept vehicle) and the Toyota Partner Robots, visitors will be introduced to the directions and technology of future society, along with the possibilities for the vehicles of the future.

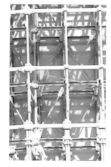

003

004

005

001-005

Zone : Corporate Pavilion Zone
Pavilion : Toyota Group Pavilion
Item : Architectural Features
Note : Structure Based on the Requisite of Reusableness
The external framework uses standard materials for light-duty steel frame coupling. The building is assembled using the newly developed friction joining construction method, which involves making as few holes for bolts and as few welds as possible in order that the materials may be reused after dismantlement.

006-008

Zone : Corporate Pavilion Zone
Pavilion : Toyota Group Pavilion
Item : Robot Performances
Note : There are two performances: a welcome show and the main show. The welcome show is a highly entertaining performance featuring robots that welcome visitors to a future world. The main show features uplifting performances involving the i-unit and i-foot robot. A fantastic spectacle will unfold on the stage by means of a giant 360-degree screen and stage props. Through the appearance onstage of elements of life, nature and future society, visitors will be introduced to the wonder of moving about freely and living, and also to a new kind of relationship between people and cars.

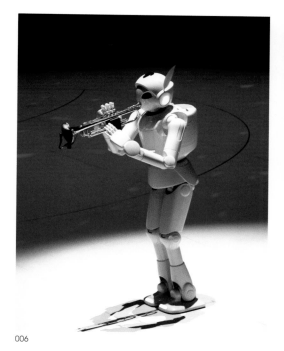

006

007

008

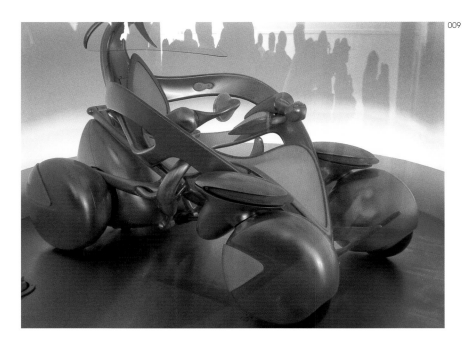

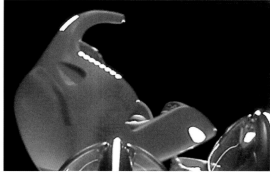

009-011
Zone : Corporate Pavilion Zone
Pavilion : Toyota Group Pavilion
Item : Robot Performances
Note : This is a lively stage for robots. The DJ robot gives performance with the host. The concept vehicle "i-unit" is light and funtional, with adorable exterior design. Visitors are eager to ride it.

001-020

Zone : Corporate Pavilion Zone

Pavilion : Mountain of Dreams

Note : Mountain of Dreams is made up of seven corporations. Its theme is "The Power of the 21st Century."

001-010

Zone : Corporate Pavilion Zone
Pavilion : Mountain of Dreams
Item : Architectural Features
Note : Four zones are housed under a single mountain-shaped roof to create a sense of unity. The mountain roof evokes images of Mt. Fuji. The height of the pavilion, including the mountain roof is over 40 m, making this a landmark within the Expo grounds.

005

006

007

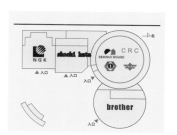

005-010

Zone : Corporate Pavilion Zone

Pavilion : Mountain of Dreams

Item : Architectural Features

Note : At nightfall, bathed in the red lighting, the 41.5-meter high mountain-shaped roof modelled on Mt.Fuji evokes the image of "Red Fuji," a woodblock print by Edo period (1603-1868) artist Katsushika Hokusai from his book Thirty-six Views of Mt. Fuji.

008

009

010

011-013

Zone : Corporate Pavilion Zone
Pavilion : Mountain of Dreams
Item : Theme Theatre "Open Your Mind"
Note : In the theme zone "Open Your Mind", comprised of Sekisui House, Chubu-Nippon Broadcasting Co., Tokai Television Broadcasting Co., and the Chunichi Shimbun , Mamoru Oshii, a world-renowned director of animated and live-action films, has created a multifaceted performance that makes use of such elements as images on the world's largest floor screen to produce a three-dimensional performance, making this the first experiential space in the history of World Expositions. The aim is to have visitors think anew about the recovery of the Earth while experiencing the wonder of nature and the environment.

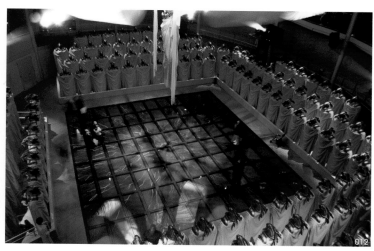

 014

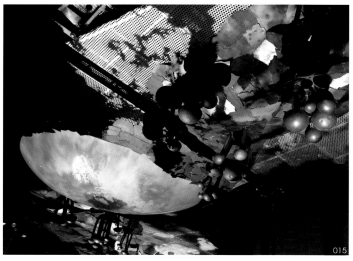 015

 016

 017

014-017

Zone : Corporate Pavilion Zone
Pavilion : Mountain of Dreams
Item : Theme Theatre "Open Your Mind"
Note : In the experiential video space made up of world's largest floor video screens, hundreds of video images about nature and living creatures are presented on the walls and overhead as well. With the combination of audio effects, human senses are stimulated. In this way, visitors are awakened to environmental problems.

018-020

Zone : Corporate Pavilion Zone
Pavilion : Mountain of Dreams
Item : Theme Theatre "Open Your Mind"
Note : In the experiential video space made up of world's largest floor video screens, hundreds of video images about nature and living creatures are presented on the walls and overhead as well. With the combination of audio effects, human senses will be stimulated. In this way, visitors will be awakened to environmental problems. During the exposition, the theme will turn into "The Sea". "The Sky", and " The Earth" in succession, on the basis of every two months, and the head of the toy figurine around the floor video screens will simultaneously change into that of the fish, the bird and the dog. The design is original.

018

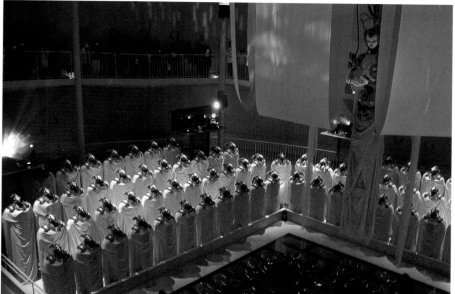

019

020

001-006

Zone : Corporate Pavilion Zone

Pavilion : Hitachi Group Pavilion

Note : The theme of this pavilion is "Nature Contact-Contact with Endangered Species Revived by Hitachi IT-." Part of the pavilion is textured to create the image of a river running through a gorge. The pavilion is powered with bifacial solar cell panels.

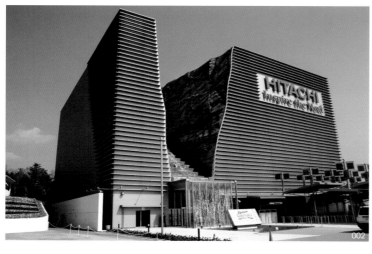

003

004

005

004-006

Zone : Corporate Pavilion Zone

Pavilion : Hitachi Group Pavilion

Item : Interactive Performances

Note : To realize "Contact with Endangered Species" IT technology such as portable terminals, Mixed Reality techniques and Hitachi patented RFID (Radio Frequency Identification) IC chip "μ-chip" is adopted to give interactive life to the endangered animals. The Adventure Scope is used that allows visitors to see endangered species revived realistically before their eyes through a "Mixed Reality" technique that combines a diorama and a CG movie. The diorama recreates the actual environment where these endangered animals live. The CG rendered the animal is revived in real time in the diorama. When visitors extend their hands to the animal, the hand sensor detects the position. The animal will approach and visitors can move it anywhere they want.

006

001-007

Zone : Corporate Pavilion Zone

Pavilion : Gas Pavilion

Note : The sponsor of this pavilion is Japan Gas Association, which consists of about 230 natural gas corporations nationwide. Its theme is "Dream Energy for People and the Earth". It enables visitors to easily understand the versatility and possibilities of natural gas, a form of clean energy that is easy on humans and the Earth, and whose increased use around the world is hoped for.

001-004

Zone : Corporate Pavilion Zone
Pavilion : Gas Pavilion
Item : Architectural Features
Note : Characteristic of this pavilion is the rhythmic cylinder composed of a series of wooden pillars and the gently sloping staircase that winds around the exterior. The wooden construction and the rooftop greenery conjure up a sense of oneness with the main corridor of the venue-the Global Loop-and the surrounding nature.

004

005

006

007

005-007

Zone : Corporate Pavilion Zone

Pavilion : Gas Pavilion

Item : Architectural Features

Note : Lighted up, the Gas Pavilion is transparent and rhythmic.

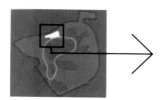

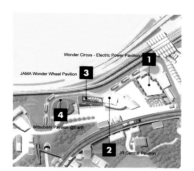

001-018

Zone : Corporate Pavilion Zone

Pavilion : Electric Power Pavilion

Note : Its theme is:" Powerful Imagination--Imagination is the energy needed to create a rich future!"The outside walls of the Wonder Circus--Electric Power Pavilion is adorned with pictures expressing kindness to people and nature that were submitted by children. The whole of the pavilion will share with the world the exchanges with and the imaginative powers of many children, who hold the future in their hands.

001

002

003-007
Zone : Corporate Pavilion Zone
Pavilion : Electric Power Pavilion
Item : Outdoor Waiting Zone: [The Circus Fountain]
Note : The space in front of the Wonder-Circus Electric Power Pavilion (roughly 1,500 m²) warmly welcomes visitors based on the theme of "Flowers, Water, Wind, and the Sun."

006

007

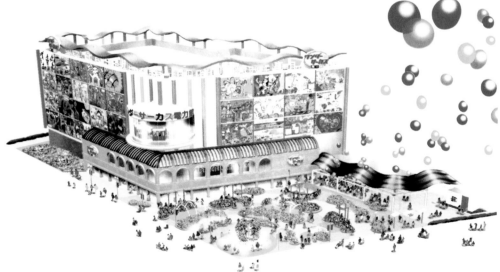

008

009

008-009

Zone : Corporate Pavilion Zone
Pavilion : Electric Power Pavilion
Item : An Electric-car Ride
Note : A train-like ride will guide visitors through eight scenes that express "Earth, Humanity, and Dreams--What a Wonderful World," based on science and technology, coexistence with nature, and the human heart.

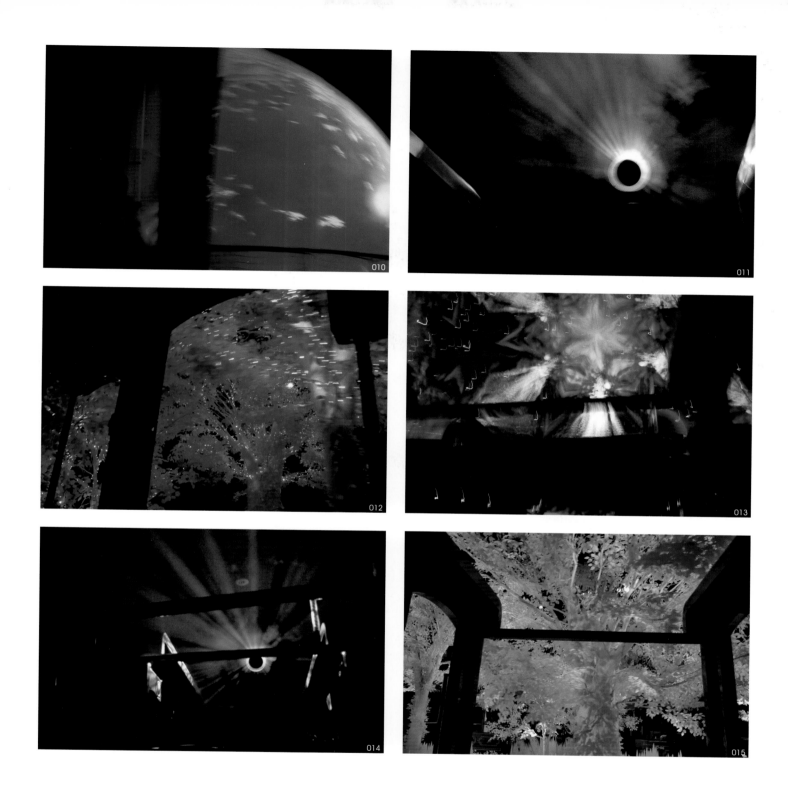

010-015

Zone : Corporate Pavilion Zone

Pavilion : Electric Power Pavilion

Item : An Electric-car Ride

Note : Riding on the electric car and enjoying beautiful scenes, one can't help marvelling at the ingenuity of Mother Nature.

016-018

Zone : Corporate Pavilion Zone
Pavilion : Electric Power Pavilion
Item : An Electric-car Ride
Note : The lanterns remind visitors of the Japanese temple fair.

016

017

018

001·005

Zone : Corporate Pavilion Zone
Pavilion : Brother
Note : This pavilion with the theme of "Output Fantasy"presents all kinds of magical robots. Visitors can have a firsthand experience of various products and technology.

003-005

Zone : Corporate Pavilion Zone

Pavilion : Brother

Item : Performances of Robots

Note : Brother Industries makes an introduction of the multilingual robot "ifbot", which can dance and talk and capable of simple dialogues. It is developed by Sekisui House/Takenaka Corp. Joint Design Team. "Ifbot" will also greet visitors and give a delightful performance with lively performers.

001-006

Zone : Corporate Pavilion Zone

Pavilion : JAMA Wonder Wheel Pavilion

Note : This exhibit features a Ferris wheel that reaches 50 meters above the ground, which is the first such attempt in the history of International Expositions. The theme of this pavilion is "People, Vehicles, and Planet Earth: Heading into the Future". Visitors will view the past, present and future of people, cars and the Earth; coexistence between nature and cars; and the possibilities, dreams and appeal of cars, which continue to evolve alongside humans.

004

005

001-006

Zone : Corporate Pavilion Zone
Pavilion : JAMA Wonder Wheel Pavilion
Item : Design of the Pavilion
Note : The red Ferris wheel with a diameter of 47 meters is eye-catching. Visitors experience a moving and mysterious world overflowing with surprises, fun and dreams during their 8-minute "Time Travel" in the Ferris wheel.

006

001-006

Zone : Corporate Pavilion Zone
Pavilion : Robot Information
Note : At the General Information Centers and the Reception desk of EXPO Association Headquarter, Robot Actriod resembling a Japanese lady in her 20s will give site information to visitors with their conversation skills in four languages (Japanese, English, Chinese, Korean).

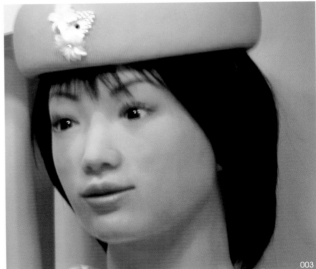

001-006

Zone : Corporate Pavilion Zone

Pavilion : Robot Information

Item : Guide Robots

Note : Actroid is developed by Japanese Kokoro Co., Ltd, and can recognize 40,000 phrases in either Japanese or Chinese or Korean or English. Her eyes and eyelashes are true to life, and lips moveable. She wears appropriate expressions in accordance with about 2,000 replies. She can cross her arms and bow to evade sensitive questions touching upon privacy. She has the sense of humor as well. There are in total 5 kinds of working and entertaining robots like Actroid, including Security Robots, Guide Robots, Sanitation Robots, Next-Generation Wheelchair Robots, and Child-Care Robots that will interactively play and talk with children, recognizing each child through their personal identification and voice identification functions. They are over 100 in number.

CHINA PAVILION

001-021

Zone : Asia Zone

Pavilion : China Pavilion

Note : Under the theme "Nature, City, Harmony - Art of Life," the exhibition aims to convey the pursuit of balanced development in China by removing discordant elements in urban and rural development and in the relationship between economic development and social issues so that man and nature can get along in harmony.

004

004-007

Zone : Asia Zone

Pavilion : China Pavilion

Item : The Tree of Life

Note : The Tree of Life refers to an elegant musical movement. Using the light effect of the Tree of Life, the exhibition presents the scenes of seasonal change and the order of day and night. Fragrance floats out of the Tree of Life and combines with the simulated sound of nature, giving visitors a novel audiovisual experience.

008-010

Zone : Asia Zone
Pavilion : China Pavilion
Item : A Tour of Chinese Civilization
Note : A tour of Chinese civilization: The large relief on the wall and video documentaries about Chinese cities give the visitor a broad sense of Chinese civilization, from antiquity to modern life.

008

009

010

011-013

Zone : Asia Zone

Pavilion : China Pavilion

Item : Art of Life: Sandalwood Study

Note : The Chinese-style study is furnished with sandalwood furniture of Qing Dynasty design. The study also serves as a VIP lounge and a place for small performances.

014-016
Zone : Asia Zone
Pavilion : China Pavilion
Item : Rhyme of Light
Note : The application of three-dimensional animation and virtual interaction, and the integration of Chinese traditional cultural symbols with modern digital technology bring to visitors magic feelings and initiates novel insights on life and art.

017

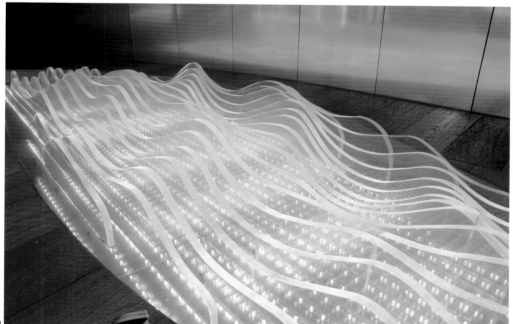

018

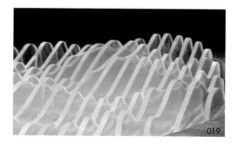

019

020

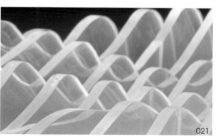

021

017-021

Zone : Asia Zone
Pavilion : China Pavilion
Item : Concept of Water
Note : LED light source and transparent organic glass etc are used to produce the effects of undulating waves and running of water, giving expression to nature, grace of water and feelings of life.

001-014

Zone : Asia Zone

Pavilion : Republic of Korea Pavilion

Note : The theme of the Korea Pavilion is "Light in Life." Here, the visitor can fully experience the Korean view of nature and outlook of life, which are blended in five traditional Korean colors - green, red, yellow, black and white. The visitor is also invited to feel the Korean culture as well as the dynamism of Korean industry.

1 Tiger in five colors
2 Korean & Five colors
3 Blue
4 Red
5 Yellow
6 Black
7 White
8 Special Exhibitions
9 Future technologies
10 3D Animation
11 Souvenir Shop
12 EXPO 2012 in Korea

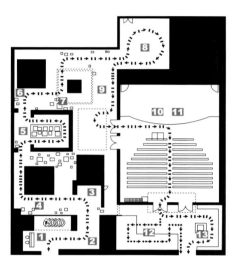

003-004

Zone : Asia Zone

Pavilion : Republic of Korea Pavilion

Item : Detail of Exhibition

Note : Bright red and the regular model have a pleasing visual effect.

003

004

005-007

Zone : Asia Zone

Pavilion : Republic of Korea Pavilion

Item : Detail of Exhibition

Note : White represents light. The traditional Korean paper is snow-white and beautiful. The huge box (6 meters by 6 meters) of Korean paper laced with traditional Korean mountain bridgework floats up to 7 meters high. Dozens of varieties of wild pressed flowers, bathed with light from the display box, vie for attention in brilliant shades of white.

008

009

010

011

008-011

Zone : Asia Zone

Pavilion : Republic of Korea Pavilion

Item : Detail of Exhibition

Note : Yellow signifies soil, the wellspring of life. Here, Korean ceramics crafted by Korean masters are on display along with a large yellow wall picture created from semiconductors.

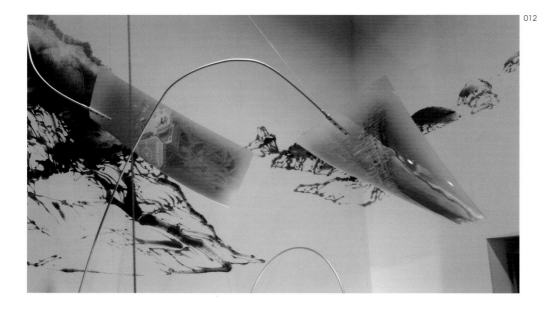

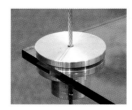

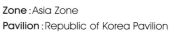

013

Zone : Asia Zone
Pavilion : Republic of Korea Pavilion
Item : Detail of Exhibition
Note : Black stands for coal, nature. Standing before a screen installed inside a black booth built with natural coal, the visitor will have the sensation of blending into the nature. In addition, the visitor can enjoy the sublime Korean nature through black-ink animated video.

014

Zone : Asia Zone
Pavilion : Republic of Korea Pavilion
Item : Digital Interactive Installation
Note : When visitors stand in front of the screen, their shadows reflecting on the screen shoot out buds. Then they come into flowers and trees grow gradually. Around the full-blown trees fly the butterflies just as flower leaves do.

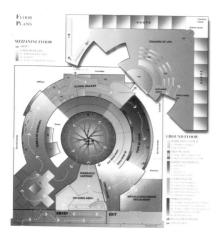

001-010

Zone : Asia Zone

Pavilion : India Pavilion

Note : The pavilion's theme is a journey to explore nature's wisdom. The thought of nature's wisdom is understood in India as a multilayered system. To express this, the pavilion's displays center on two well-known symbols of the Bodhi Tree and the Dharmachakra.

001

002

001

Zone : Asia Zone

Pavilion : India Pavilion

Item : Exterior Design

Note : There are several artificial trees in the frame-shaped structure on the gate of India pavilion. The leaves are made of special materials, lifelike and colorful against various background colors. The trees catch the eye. Especially when they are lighted up in the evening, the trees will bring forth dreamlike feelings.

003-005

Zone : Asia Zone

Pavilion : India Pavilion

Item : Detail of Exhibition

Note : The Bodhi Tree means respect for nature by the Indian people and an eternal symbol for love and worship. A tree towering at the center of the pavilion depicts the Bodhi Tree under which Buddha achieved enlightenment.

Combination of lighting and images give birth to the peculiar Bodhi Tree.

006-010

Zone : Asia Zone

Pavilion : India Pavilion

Item : Internal Design

Note : In the center of this pavilion stands the Treelight, and on the ceiling, there is a sun made of traditional Indian cloth. The daturas and market scenes are a feast for the eyes. Well-known for its IT technology, there will also be relevant displays.

001-005

Zone : Asia Zone

Pavilion : Saudi Arabia Pavilion

Note : Through exhibitions with the theme of "wisdom, harmony and hope," Saudi Arabia hopes visitors will feel the wisdom of Islamic culture about the natural environment and deepen understanding about Islam.

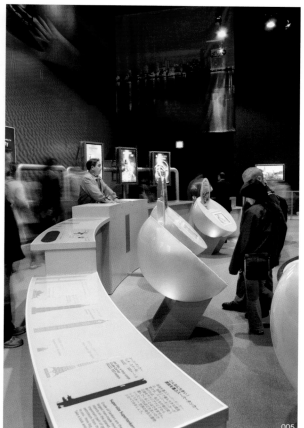

003-005

Zone : Asia Zone

Pavilion : Saudi Arabia Pavilion

Item : Detail of Exhibition

Note : Desert country Saudi Arabia is not only abundant in oil and natural gas, but also a charming land that has created glorious history and is destined to have a bright future. Exhibition of its unique culture ang significant achievements has been set in the desert scenery.

001-005

Zone : Asia Zone

Pavilion : Nepal Pavilion

Note : Through the work of over 200 craftsmen, Buddhist temples in Nepal have been reproduced. The focal point of the pavilion is the Mandala, which symbolically represents the Cosmos. The Mandala has been used in Nepal since time immemorial as the basis and tool for planning and designing temples, palaces and simple residences, as well as entire cities.

003·005

Zone : Asia Zone

Pavilion : Nepal Pavilion

Item : The Exterior and Interior

Note : Nepal is located by the Himalayas. Hinduism is its national religion. Religion has a profound influence on all the aspects of life in this country, which can be easily noticed in its architectural decorations and various products.

001·006

Zone : Asia Zone

Pavilion : Qatar Pavilion

Note : The pure and elegant white, and the pointed arch decorative corridor are the first impressions of Qatar. The theme of Qatar Pavilion is "balanced development of the old and the new." While Qatar has the desert culture with dramatic sand dunes, falconry and the Bedouin way of life, the country at the same time has the sea culture such as fishing and pearling in the Persian Gulf.

004-006

Zone : Asia Zone

Pavilion : Qatar Pavilion

Item : The Exterior and Interior

Note : Qadar is situated on the southwest coast of Persian Gulf. Saudi Arabia and United Arab Emirates are its neighbors. Under the influence of tropical desert climate, it is hot and dry, except for the coastal areas. The variation of seasons is not noticeable. The majority of its population believe in Islamism. The Gatar Pavilion is of Islamic style.

001

Zone : Asia Zone
Pavilion : Yemen Pavilion
Item : Exterior Design
Note : The exhibition focuses on the re-creation of Sana'a streets and videos of Socotra Island, regarded as the Galapagos of the Indian Ocean. The island is home to an abundance of unique flora and fauna, forming its own ecosystem.

002

Zone : Asia Zone
Pavilion : Iran Pavilion
Item : Exterior of the Pavilion
Note : The concept of organizing the pavilion is based on the sub-theme "Art of Life." The contents are the examples of ancient monuments, archeological masterpieces of art and architecture, traditional music and poetry, the skillful artisans weaving handmade carpets and kelims and producing other crafts, and the ancient irrigation and cooling systems working throughout history.

001

002

003-004

Zone : Asia Zone

Pavilion : Sri Lanka Pavilion

Item : The Exterior and Interior

Note : The exhibition aims to introduce Sri Lanka as a cradle of unique natural setting and unique religious and cultural achievements with a historical glory of creating unique art and architecture through Theravada Buddhist practice.The key exhibit depicting a full-size model of a typical traditional village Buddhist shrine on pillars built with timber and mud containing three statues of Buddha is very impressive. Its walls are painted with events from Buddha's life and Jataka Stories relating previous births of Buddha.

003

004

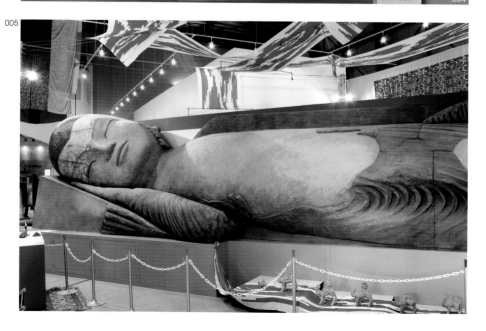

005

005

Zone : Asia Zone

Pavilion : Central Asia Pavilion

Item : The Interior

Note : The Central Asia Pavilion dynamically presents the cultural exchanges between East and West under the theme "Exchanges of Time." The main exhibit is a replica of a reclining Buddha unearthed in 1966 during archaeological excavations of the Ajina-Tepa hill, the site of an ancient monastery on a Silk Road branch connecting Central Asia with India. This supine Buddha, known as "Buddha in Nirvana," is said to date back to the 6th century.

Europe & Mediterranean Zone

Germany
France
Turkey
Spain
Italy
Greece
Jordan Pavilion
Croatia
Morocco
Tunisia

001-012

Zone : Europe & Mediterranean Zone
Pavilion : Germany
Note : The theme of the German pavilion is "Bionis" proposing coexistence between nature and technology. "Bionis" is named after bionics, a study to apply natural principles to technology. Based on a communication-oriented concept, the pavilion is an experience type with minimal explanations, enabling visitors to get fresh firsthand knowledge.

001-002

Zone : Europe & Mediterranean Zone
Pavilion : Germany
Item : Optimized structures
Note : The visitor faces 2 optimized structures: One is the 3D cut away slice of a bird's bone; the other is a genuine Inner Leading Edge Rib from an A380. At a terminal, the visitor is placed in the role of an EADS Engineer. He/she can optimize a wing structures and witness the benefits achieved thanks to this optimized construction: lower weight meaning lower fuel consumption, improved freight capacities, longer haul, lower costs etc.

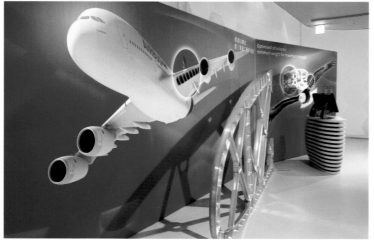

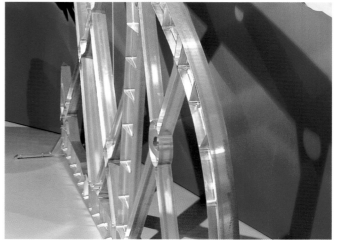

003-004

Zone : Europe & Mediterranean Zone
Pavilion : Germany
Item : The Lotus-Effect
Note : Biomimetic Self-cleaning Surfaces: The surface of a gigantic artificial lotus blossom is sprayed with paint in order to demonstrate the self-cleaning properties of its petals.

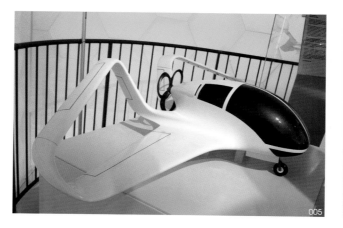

005-006

Zone : Europe & Mediterranean Zone
Pavilion : Germany
Item : "Loop"
Note : A model of an ultralight aircraft (UL) with looped box-wing construction and looped propellers.

007
Zone : Europe & Mediterranean Zone
Pavilion : Germany
Item : Interior Design

008-009
Zone : Europe & Mediterranean Zone
Pavilion : Germany
Item : Detail of the Exhibition
Note : Engineering components grow like trees
and bones.
The computer simulation of biological growth
by Prof. Dr. Claus Mattheck helps to shape-
optimize engineering structures regarding
maximum strength and minimum weight.

010

Zone : Europe & Mediterranean Zone
Pavilion : Germany
Item : Detail of the Exhibition
Note : Shark skin reduces turbulent drag. Now, sharks have moved into the focus of modern fluid dynamics. According to relevant research, the skin of a fast-swimming shark is covered with tiny tooth-like scales, called denticles, which give it a rough, sand-paper-like texture. When transferring this mechanism to technical surfaces, a drag reduction of 5-10 % can be achieved, which increases speed or contributes to fuel saving. Nowadays, makers of swimming suits also try to mimic the shark skin effect with their products.

011

Zone : Europe & Mediterranean Zone
Pavilion : Germany
Item : Model of the Glider
Note : The model of the glider displays important milestones in our pursuit of flying.

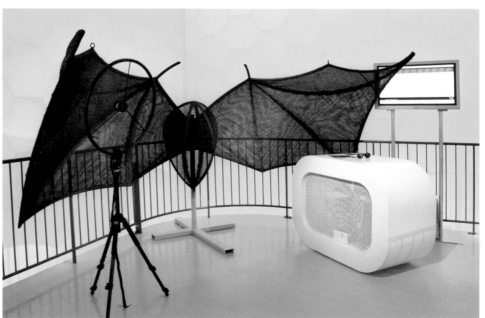

012

Zone : Europe & Mediterranean Zone
Pavilion : Germany
Item : Detail of the Exhibition
Note : Acoustic Camera - simplifies noise analysis. Inspired by the barn owl, the acoustic camera simplifies noise analysis. Barn owls can locate their prey - little mice - also under deep snowy surfaces and in complete darkness. They hunt them by means of their very sensitive ears. The owl's brain processes a virtual noise image of the environment.

FRANCE

001-008

Zone : Europe & Mediterranean Zone
Pavilion : France
Note : France interprets in its own way the EXPO 2005 theme "Nature's Wisdom," and questions visitors about "sustainable development." Designs at the pavilion are free and open, offering an atmosphere to warmly wrap visitors with calm light and warm colors.

001

002

Zone : Europe & Mediterranean Zone
Pavilion : France
Item : Detail of the Exhibition
Note : The interactive device is made up of the giant bulb and gigantic button.

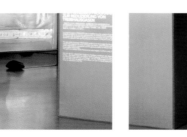

002

003

Zone : Europe & Mediterranean Zone

Pavilion : France

Item : Interactive Forum: What Concern Us?

Note : Located at the center of the pavilion, the interactive installation "What Concern Us?" proposes a new form of relationship between man and nature with simple images. Capted by cameras, the visitors are followed by individual lights. Their presence and movements in this large space triggers the apparition of 12 videos, and hundreds of questions about sustained development.

001\004

Zone : Europe & Mediterranean Zone

Pavilion : France

Item : Interior Design

Note : The theatre made up of hundreds of thousands of semi-circular salt blocks is attractive, whose lighting effects change under the control of computer programs. The interior of the theatre is like a labyrinth, full of screens. Visitors are immersed in the world of video images here.

005

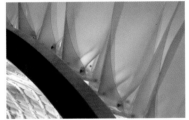
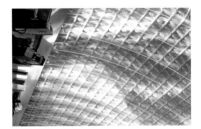

005-008

Zone : Europe & Mediterranean Zone
Pavilion: France
Item : The Abstract Model Created by Dassault Systems
Note : This huge echinus-shaped glittering model that keeps changing its color is the work of Dassault Systems from France. The screen in the model uses a 3D simulation to illustrate the process of completing this "object of imagination".

001-007

Zone : Europe & Mediterranean Zone
Pavilion : Turkey
Note : The Turkey Pavilion focuses on considering the problem of forests rapidly disappearing from the Earth due to destructive development and climate changes.

001

002

003-005

Zone : Europe & Mediterranean Zone
Pavilion : Turkey
Item : Interior Design
Note : The pavilion has been built with recyclable timber. It is a traditional Turkish-Islamic structure with a wide space, featured with a geometrical motif like snow crystals.

003

004

005

007

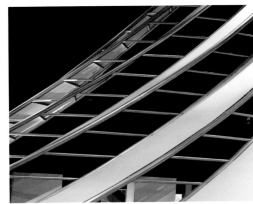

006-007

Zone : Europe & Mediterranean Zone
Pavilion : Turkey
Item : Interior Design
Note : Entering the Turkey Pavilion, visitors are attracted by its exhibition shelves at once.

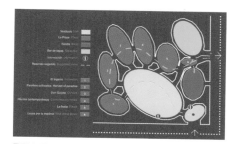

001-016

Zone : Europe & Mediterranean Zone
Pavilion : Spain
Note : The Spanish Pavilion's theme is "Sharing the Art and Wisdom of Life." The pavilion is built by noted Spanish architect Alejandro Zaera-Polo.

001

001-002

Zone : Europe & Mediterranean Zone
Pavilion : Spain
Item : The Exterior of the Building
Note : The pavilion reproduces a traditional lattice window on its external wall. This wall, made by geometrically piling up six-sided earthenware blocks made in Spain and transported to Japan, is 1.5 meters away from the pavilion and is corridor for visitors. By softening the sunlight and preventing winds and rain, the wall has the effect of making the inside and outside unclear.

002

003-005

Zone : Europe & Mediterranean Zone
Pavilion : Spain
Item : Interior Design
Note : The whole pavilion has been designed with a Christian cathedral as an image, and visitors can go from a wide event space called "Plaza" imitating the central corridor of a cathedral to five exhibition spaces, each called a "chapel." The chapels around the Plaza where 16 screens are situated on the walls over the heads of visitors were designed by different architects and artists.

006-008

Zone : Europe & Mediterranean Zone
Pavilion : Spain
Item : "Innovation"
Note : The first theme is "Innovation" reproducing Spain's Astrobiology Center, which is studying the origin of life on Mars. There, a replica of a robot operated by remote control in Spanish mines welcomes visitors.

006

007

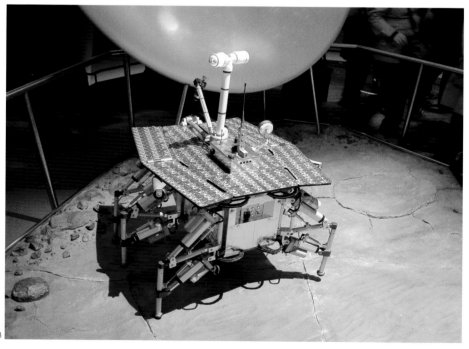

008

009-010

Zone : Europe & Mediterranean Zone
Pavilion : Spain
Item : "World of Don Quixote."
Note : The theme of this chapel is the "World of Don Quixote." Exhibits related to the novel, which celebrates its 400th publishing anniversary this year, and other Spanish classic works of literature are shown. Videos and interactive multi-media book models are available.

009

010

011

012

011-013

Zone : Europe & Mediterranean Zone
Pavilion : Spain
Item : "Contemporary Heroes "
Note : Under the theme of "Contemporary heroes," many Spanish athletes are introduced. This chapel celebrates highly admired Spanish sports figures, along with famous Spanish festivals.

013

014

Zone : Europe & Mediterranean Zone
Pavilion : Spain
Item : "Harvest of Paradise"
Note : The theme of this chapel is "Harvest of paradise." Javier Mariscal, who designed the 1992 Barcelona Olympics' official mascot "Cobi," creates a series of amazing sculptures inspired by famous Spanish food products. In addition, scenes of a Spanish market full of liveliness are restored.

015-016

Zone : Europe & Mediterranean Zone
Pavilion : Spain
Item : Design of the Shopping Area

001-020

Zone : Europe & Mediterranean Zone
Pavilion : Italy
Note : The Italian pavilion's theme is the "Italian Lifestyle." Beauty, art, culture and other Italian lifestyles are introduced under the unified theme of the "Mediterranean Sea." The pavilion is made up of three halls.

004

004-008

Zone : Europe & Mediterranean Zone

Pavilion : Italy

Item : The Interior

Note : In the first hall, "Italy full of living pleasure and life force" will be introduced. The elements used are light (a powerful, warm solar light), a large sheet of water, and glass-the glass of the walls, the gangway crossing the sheet of water and the supports used for the objects, coloured glass of varying transparency selected in such a way as to create a poetic and even oneiric effect. After crossing a bridge over the surface of water, visitors can see various exhibited items, such as objects appearing from the water's surface and objects hanging in the air-like a sequence of brightly coloured theatre wings.

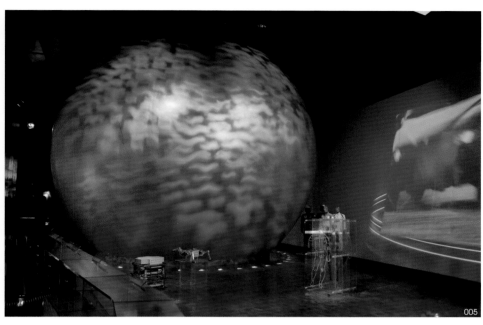

008

009

010

009
Zone : Europe & Mediterranean Zone
Pavilion : Italy
Item : Modeling with Light and Shadow
Note : Lighting and shadow give birth to the vivid portraits on the wall.

011

010
Zone : Europe & Mediterranean Zone
Pavilion : Italy
Item : Detail of the Exhibition
Note : The car is made of chocolate.

012

013

014

011-014

Zone : Europe & Mediterranean Zone
Pavilion : Italy
Item : Detail of the Exhibition
Note : The shiny Italian handicrafts embody post-modernism.

Zone : Europe & Mediterranean Zone
Pavilion : Italy
Item : Detail of the Exhibition
Note : Italian handiwork and industrial products are famous around the world. Visitors feast their eyes here.

015

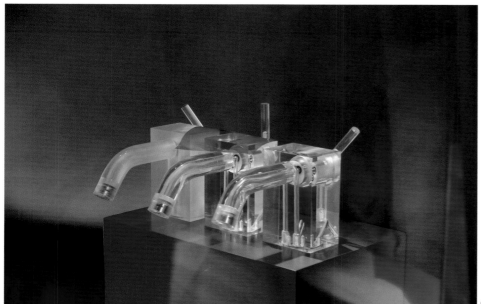

016

017

018

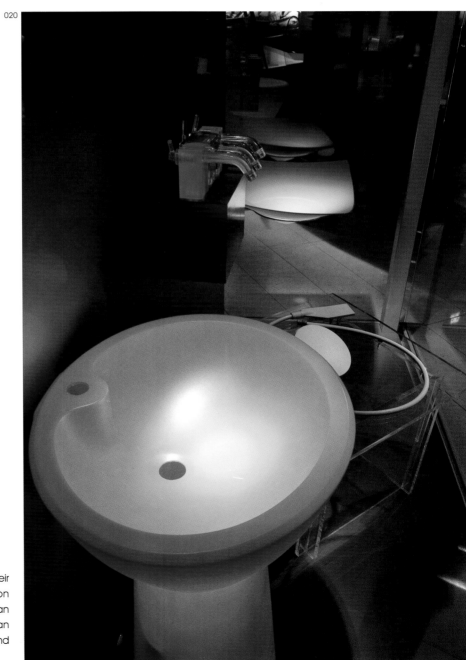

019-020

Zone : Europe & Mediterranean Zone
Pavilion : Italy
Item : Interior Design
Note : This room is dedicated to Italy's regions with their rich blend of culture and tradition. The exhibition itinerary will wind up with a reproduction of the Italian home, a warm, welcoming place that people can recognise all over the world thanks to its modern and functional design.

GREECE

001-017

Zone : Europe & Mediterranean Zone
Pavilion : Greece
Note : The theme of the Greek Pavilion is man and nature. In the pavilion, four zones are created, each symbolizing traditional cosmic factors - soil, wind, water and fire. In viewing each zone and getting in touch with the Greek nature and culture, you can enjoyably experience how this country has been harmonizing with nature since ancient times.

004-006

Zone : Europe & Mediterranean Zone
Pavilion : Greece
Item : Earth Zone
Note : As visitors enter the main presentation areas, they follow an upward path which goes through an "olive grove" built by elements in the shape of olive leaves. The presentation is carried out by texts supported by audiovisual media. Projections and presentations in this zone are made on Plasma / LCD screens and overhead projectors, and focus on the program for the protection of the environment.

007-010

Zone : Europe & Mediterranean Zone

Pavilion : Greece

Item : Air and Light Zone

Note : As visitors walk along the predetermined path, they enter a temple which is an architectural reference to the "sklepeion" The white environment refers to the clarity of thought, to the health. "Healthy mind in healthy body."Withinthis zone, visitors get acquainted with the elements of the Uranus -he Sky-the Winds and the Sun, which are all presented by Aeolos and Apollo.

011-012

Zone : Europe & Mediterranean Zone
Pavilion : Greece Pavilion
Item : Water Zone
Note : Upon arrival at the peak of the upward path, the visitor is under a large domed ceiling and a curved semicircular setting with a glass floor. A "blue" thematic environment is created here by means of special lighting effects and multi-angle projections on the surface of the dome and on the glass areas.

013-014

Zone : Europe & Mediterranean Zone
Pavilion : Greece
Item : Zone of Fire
Note : Upon arrival at the fire zone, which is related to passion, art and civilization, the visitor is immersed once again in an environment of pictures and illustrations, colors and life. A symbolic ancient theatre placed in a sectional plan on the wall, is used as a screen to project an ancient choreographic performance, which creates the impression to the spectator that he or she is watching from a higher position. The amphitheatre symbolizes the harmonic coexistence of nature and civilization over time.

015

Zone : Europe & Mediterranean Zone
Pavilion : Greece
Item : Olympic Flame
Note : Upon the visitor's exit from the "sklepeion" they arrive at a small zone where the "Olympic Flame" is projected. In this plain but impressive zone, the "Olympic Torch" of the Athens 2004 Olympic Games is mounted on a glass, illuminated wall. The names and dates of all the Olympic Games have been carved on this wall, from the antiquity until today, thus, marking the Games as the longest-lasting cultural event in the world which was born in Greece.

016-017

Zone : Europe & Mediterranean Zone
Pavilion : Greece
Item : Interactive Zone
Note : Walking out of the Fire Zone, visitors enter through a Gate an interactive zone of Greek Themes. As visitors approach the last zones of the Pavilion, they pass through kiosks which host and project themes relating to the contemporary life, tourism, products, etc.

001

001-007
Zone : Europe & Mediterranean Zone
Pavilion : Jordan Pavilion
Note : The theme is "Silent Floatation." Jordan Pavilion offers to look into the Dead Sea, called a "mini universe" with a unique ecosystem, and its relations with mankind over 5,000 years.

002

003

004

005-007

Zone : Europe & Mediterranean Zone
Pavilion : Jordan Pavilion
Item : Interior Design
Note : Within the pavilion, a module (black box) 18 meters long and wide, and 9 meters high has been created to reproduce the environment of the Dead Sea with water and sand brought from there. Visitors can have a unique experience of "not sinking." The narrow pool with nearby stones, sand and the sands and land realized by special light effects represents unique features of Jordan and reminds visitors of the fact that the Dead Sea is constantly diminishing as well.

007

001-006

Zone : Europe & Mediterranean Zone
Pavilion : Croatia
Note : The theme of the Croatia Pavilion is "A Drop of Water · a Grain of Salt. " The "salt pans" hold up a mirror to scenery and history in Croatia. Salt symbolizes moderation and hardworking of the Croatian, and it also embodies the wisdom of nature.

005

004-005
Zone : Europe & Mediterranean Zone
Pavilion : Croatia
Item : The Interior
Note : Salt, a spice and natural preservative, represents wisdom and symbolizes moderation and purity. On the first floor of the pavilion, a tour image of breaking through the sea surface from under the sea to an upper part is presented, making us remember the potentiality of the sea through ancient salt-making techniques.

006
Zone : Europe & Mediterranean Zone
Pavilion : Croatia
Item : The Interior
Note : From the second floor of the pavilion, visitors can enjoy pictures from Croatia projected from the ceiling and screened on the first floor that is covered by white salt. Visitors feel as if they are flying over Croatia with these bird's-eye video images taken from a plane of its scenery, the sea, cities, and the people and cultures.

001-005

Zone : Europe & Mediterranean Zone

Pavilion : Morocco

Note : With the theme of "Openness and Tolerance - the Sources of Moroccan Culture," the pavilion exhibits Moroccan art via a variety of materials. At the same time, wood, copper, pottery, rugs and other handicrafts are sold. At the pavilion, plasma screens show clips on nature, environment and tourism.

001

001-006

Zone : Europe & Mediterranean Zone
Pavilion : Tunisia
Note : The theme of the Tunisia Pavilion is "Tunisia: Peace and Sustainable Development." Economic development should not damage the present environment. The pavilion introduces in various exhibited materials how Tunisia is protecting and managing water and other natural resources.

002

003

002-003

Zone : Europe & Mediterranean Zone

Pavilion : Tunisia

Item : Interior Exhibition

Note : You cannot miss the introduction of Tunisian history 3,000 years long and its national land. You can also learn about the influence given by various historical stages to Tunisia - the Carthaginian, Roman, Arabian and Ottoman Turkish periods, and see the deserts, the Mediterranean Sea, oases, and rich greenery of olive and pine trees on the beach.

004

005

006

Europe Zone

United Kindom of Great Britain and Northern Ireland
Switzerland
Russian Federation
Austria
Belgium
Poland
The Netherlands
Portugal
Ireland
Czech Republic
Lithuania
Romania
Nordic Pavilion

001-011

Zone : Europe Zone
Pavilion : United Kindom of Great Britain and Northern Ireland
Note : The U.K. Pavilion exhibits garden, art and innovative technologies utilizing nature under the watchwords of "Planet of Blessing and Sprouting."

001

001-004

Zone : Europe Zone

Pavilion : United Kindom of Great Britain and Northern Ireland

Item : The External Design

Note : In front of the pavilion there is a yard, full of grasses, trees and flowers. The walls of the yard are hollowed-out with leaf patterns, so visitors can get a glimpse of the yard from outside. With green lighting in the evening, the British garden scenery is enchanting.

In the "leaf pick-up area", visitors can casually pick up a leaf-shaped card as a souvenir.

The pink bird boxes containing stunning images of the UK beauty spots have also been very popular.

002

003

004

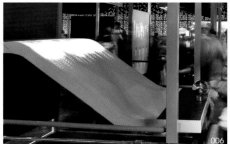

005-006

Zone : Europe Zone
Pavilion : United Kindom of Great Britain and Northern Ireland
Item : Interactive Installation
Note : Visitors can simply rock the control lever to mobilize the projected words.

007-010

Zone : Europe Zone
Pavilion : United Kindom of Great Britain and Northern Ireland
Item : Interactive Installation
Note : With the digital interactive installation, the bees under the sunflower (words projected from the ceiling) fly with the move of lever adorned with sunflowers under the control of visitors.

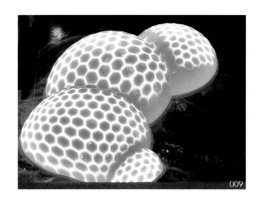

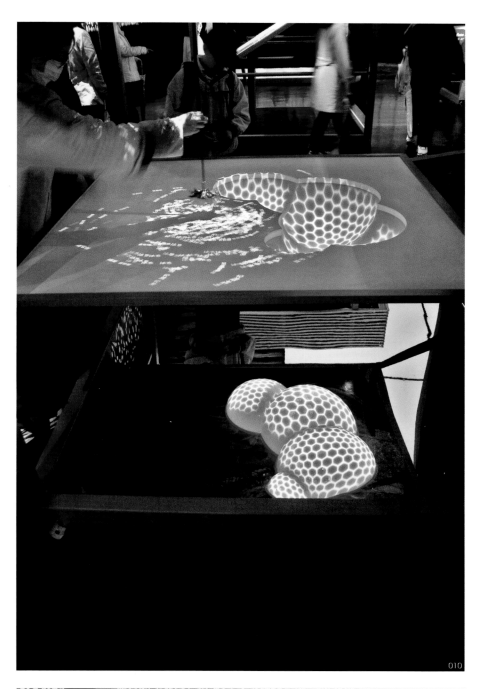

010

011

Zone : Europe Zone

Pavilion : United Kindom of Great Britain and Northern Ireland

Item : Interactive Installation

Note : When visitors do the action of swimming, the inductor will deliver this message to the computer and the fish projected by the projector connected with the computer will move about accordingly.

The interactive exhibits in the main hall are hugely popular. Visitors operate the installations and learn more about holo natIIre has inspired us in the areas of scientific discovery and the arts. They can experience a unique mix of art and science through a series of British innovations.

011

001-006

Zone : Europe Zone
Pavilion : Switzerland
Note : The theme of the Swiss Pavilion is "The Mountain" that represents the country's coexistence with nature.

001

002

001

Zone : Europe Zone
Pavilion : Switzerland
Item : The Interior
Note : The interior of the mountains features five large, transparent bubbles that represent thematic sections. Visitors to be admitted to these sections in groups of 15 are provided with talking machines - a remodeled version of the Swiss Army's flashlight. When light is turned on an exhibit, the flashlight gives information by voice in Japanese or English. Walking through dimly lit exhibition areas with a flashlight in hand, visitors will feel as if exploring an unknown world.

003

002-004

Zone : Europe Zone

Pavilion : Switzerland

Item : Internal Exhibition Hall

Note : A huge, computer-generated and printed membrane covering a frame in the shape of a high mountain range is stretched to reproduce a natural mountain range inside the pavilion.

004

005

006

001-007

Zone : Europe Zone

Pavilion : Russian Federation

Note : The theme of the Russian Federation exhibition is "Harmony of the Noosphere," which seeks to promote intelligent human societies that can live in harmony with Mother Nature.

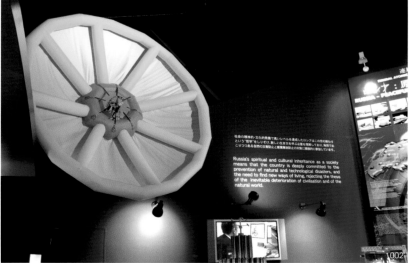

001-002

Zone : Europe Zone

Pavilion : Russian Federation

Item : Exhibition

Note : The exhibits display projects developed in Russia to promote thermonuclear and hydrogen power generation and uses of non-conventional sources of energy.

003-005

Zone : Europe Zone
Pavilion : Russian Federation
Item : Display of the Mammoth
Note : For visitors who want to take a closer look at an animal that lived more than 10,000 years ago, there is a full-size skeleton of an adult mammoth put together by paleontologists after many years of studies from remains of these prehistoric animals in Yakutia, Northern Siberia.

003

004

005

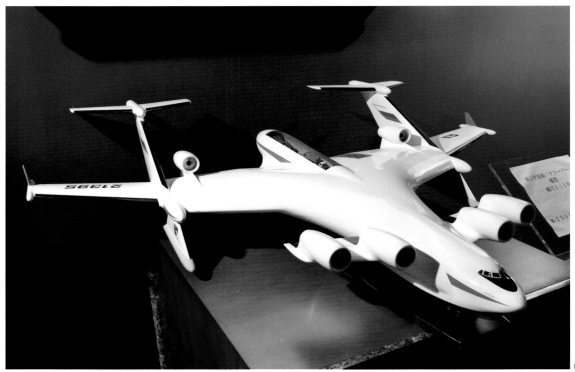

006

007

006-007

Zone : Europe Zone

Pavilion : Russian Federation

Item : Display of Space Technology

Note : Visitors can learn how it feels to be in an orbiting spacecraft by sitting in a simulator of an astronaut's workstation of a reusable space system known as C-XXI. This and other unique exhibits demonstrate the latest achievements and perspectives of the space development in Russia.

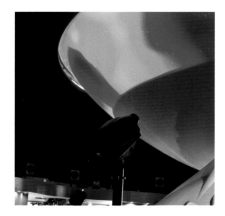

001-007
Zone : Europe Zone
Pavilion : Austria
Note : The theme is "The Art of Living". Three concrete aspects of life and areas of excellence are presented, where Austria is amongst the best in the world.

001

002

003-004

Zone : Europe Zone
Pavilion : Austria
Item : Internal Exhibition Hall
Note : The main attraction of the Austrian Pavilion is "The Slope" - an innovative prime example of Austrian wood construction, a central area, a forum for activities and interaction for numerous events. "The Slope" is a stage for Austrian life culture and achievements. But it is also an appealing invitation to visitors from the entire world to take off for Austria.

003

004

005

006

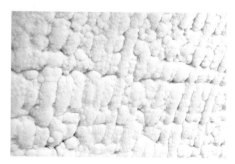

005-007
Zone : Europe Zone
Pavilion : Austria
Item : Internal Exhibition Hall
Note : The snow bar can be found in a completely white winter room, whose walls are partly covered by ice. The shock of the cold transforms the space, mood and acoustics. Austria can be "felt" here in the true sense of the word.

007

001-004

Zone : Europe Zone
Pavilion : Belgium
Note : The Belgium Pavilion tells the story of the look that Belgian artists, from Van Eyck to contemporary designers, cast on the nature around them.

002

001

001-002

Zone : Europe Zone
Pavilion : Belgium
Item : Full-view Movie
Note : This is a really innovative video projected in a 270° panorama, which employs a unique high-definition multi-camera shooting system entirely eliminating the black image-separation stripes that have been needed in every previous film of this sort.

003

004

003-004

Zone : Europe Zone
Pavilion : Belgium
Item : "Pictorial Opera"
Note : The "Pictorial Opera" of the Belgian Pavilion is to take you on a virtual tour through well over 600 years of Belgian art and creativity. The sound and light show will tell you more about how Belgian artists looked at nature and how they used the reality that surrounded them in their art.

001-006

Zone : Europe Zone

Pavilion : Poland

Note : The main theme of Polish participation in EXPO 2005 is "See the Beauty" - that is, beauty in many aspects, such as the beauty of nature, wise coexistence of civilization and nature, art and freedom of creation, and artistic works deeply inspired by nature.

001

002

001-004

Zone : Europe Zone

Pavilion : Poland

Item : External Design

Note : The elevation of the pavilion is defined by means of state-of-the-art computer technique and fully innovative technology based on a modular system of spatially arched steel frames with white wicker wound around them. It depicts the dynamic and at the same time sustainable development of contemporary Poland where state-of-the-art technology and modern art are matched with tradition and ecology.

005-006

Zone : Europe Zone

Pavilion : Poland

Item : Internal Exhibition

Note : In the section called "Wieliczka", visitors have a chance to encounter the unique atmosphere of the most famous and most beautiful Polish salt mine. For that purpose the walls of the room are made of original blocks of salt brought from Poland. There is a multi-media presentation here.

001-008

Zone : Europe Zone
Pavilion : The Netherlands
Note : To a large extent, water defines what the Netherlands looks like today. Therefore, the Netherlands has chosen "Land of Water" as the central theme for EXPO 2005.

001-005

Zone : Europe Zone

Pavilion : The Netherlands

Item : External Design

Originality Background : The Netherlands Pavilion has an impressive exterior facade - a "Delft Blue" tile structure (with blue images on white tiles) and gigantic tulips casually hanging out from the side of the pavilion.

006-008

Zone : Europe Zone

Pavilion : The Netrerlands

Item : "Holland: Land of Water"

Note : The atrium has a huge pond at the center, which functions as a complete side-to-side media surface. Visitors are invited to gather around the pond to enjoy an audiovisual presentation about "Holland: Land of Water" for about seven minutes. This presentation will depict the importance of a balance between man and nature from the unique viewpoint of the Netherlands, which has constantly grappled with challenges on the boundary between land and water. As such, it throws light on a quintessential balance between man and nature, and between land and water through the Netherlands' involvement with water.

006

007

008

001-006
Zone : Europe Zone
Pavilion : Portugal
Note : The theme adopted in the exhibition is
"Nature and History: Portugal where the land ends
and the sea begins."

001-002
Zone : Europe Zone
Pavilion : Portugal
Item : Exterior Façade
Note : The variation of the width of decorative sheets on the exterior façade
produces the effect of undulating movement.

003

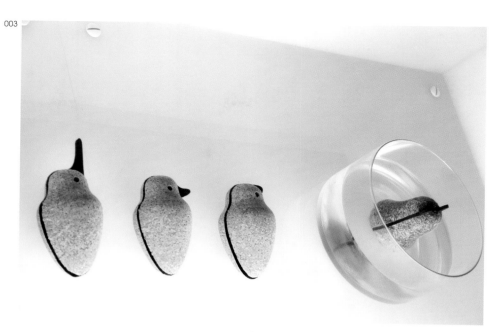

004

003-006
Zone : Europe Zone
Pavilion : Portugal
Item : Design of Products

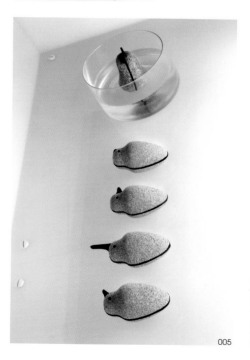

005

006

001-004

Zone : Europe Zone

Pavilion : Ireland

Note : The theme of the Ireland Pavilion is "Art of Life." The pavilion exhibits rich Celtic art and cultural heritage together.

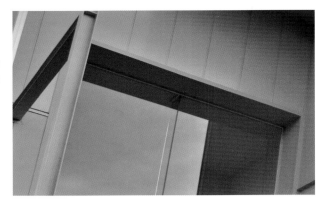

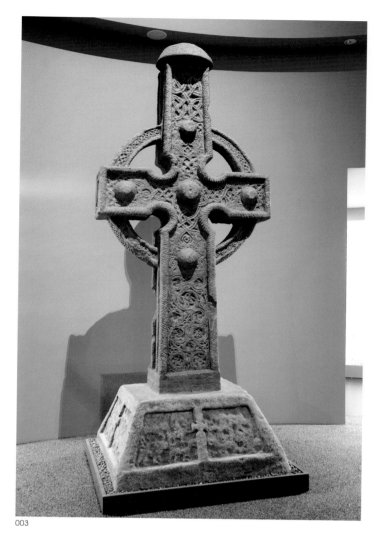

003

004

003-004

Zone : Europe Zone

Pavilion : Ireland

Item : Internal Exhibition

Note : The principal feature of the pavilion is an exhibit of six of the "High Crosses of Ireland." The replicas of these stone monuments were originally created by the National Museum of Ireland 100 years ago and have never been displayed overseas. Towering up to 7 meters tall, these symbols from the past create a powerful impression.

001-011
Zone : Europe Zone
Pavilion : Czech Republic
Note : The Czech Pavilion's theme is "The Art of Life." Thus, it focuses on art in the belief that art can bring countries and different cultures closer together because in modern society, art is the universal language that transcends spoken languages to express emotions.

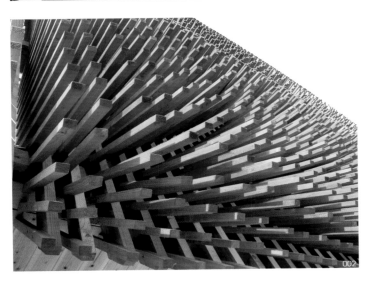

004-006

Zone : Europe Zone
Pavilion : Czech Republic
Item : Entrance of the Pavilion

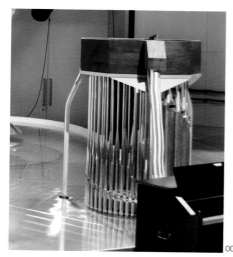

004

005

006

007

008

007-008

Zone : Europe Zone

Pavilion : Czech Republic

Item : Internal Exhibition

Note : Under the banner of "The Garden of Fantasy and Music," the Czech Pavilion brings music and visuals into full play, enabling visitors to see, hear, touch and feel the exhibits, such as a water piano, "voices" of metal, wood and stone, and a light trumpet. Visitors will be introduced to Czech culture and society through the exhibits and events that appeal to their senses and hearts.

009

Zone : Europe Zone

Pavilion : Czech Republic

Item : Lighting and Shadow Presentation Device

Note : The insect samples placed in the revolving glass semi-spherical ball make their appearance focalizing on the wall by turn with the lighting and the movement of the center glass ball.

009

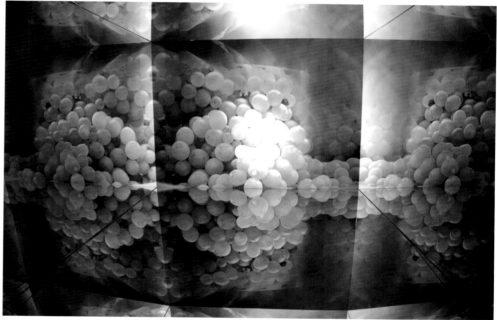

010

011

010-011

Zone : Europe Zone

Pavilion : Czech Republic

Item : Kaleidoscope

Note : With the effects of a kaleidoscope, you may feel kind of lost with the overwhelming video images.

001-008

Zone : Europe Zone

Pavilion : Lithuania

Note : Ancient yet modern, Lithuania is taking part in a world
exposition in Japan for the first time. The theme of the
exhibition is "Lithuania: progress of civilization and culture."

001

002

003-005

Zone : Europe Zone
Pavilion : Lithuania
Item : The Three-dimension Spiral-shaped DNA Model
Note : The most eye-catching exhibit is a three-dimension spiral-shaped DNA model. It is here that the Lithuanian civilization and culture and Lithuanian natural scenery are shown on screens. Once visitors finish watching the three Lithuanian movies, "Journey Throughout Lithuania," "Good morning. Made in Lithuania" and "Breeze from Lithuania," they will have a pretty good idea of the way of life in the Baltic state.

006

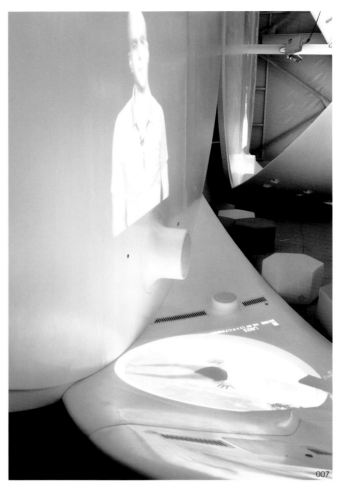

007

008

001-006
Zone : Europe Zone
Pavilion : Romania
Note : The theme of the exhibition is "Legacy to the Future."
There are glass mirrors in the frame at its facade, which
can turn around and thus reflects scenes and people at
the pavilion gate.

004-006
Zone: Europe Zone
Pavilion: Romania
Item: Interior Design
Note: The concept of interior design is based on the idea of combining exhibition space with space for artistic performance. A wooden water mill, 6 meters in diameter, is located on the right side of the pavilion in a pool. When visitors pass through the turnstiles, via traditional wooden mechanisms, the movement is transmitted to the wheel. Folkloric costumes circle the pavilion wall in a slow movement similar to the traditional Romanian dance "hora," conveying the same impression.

001-006

Zone : Europe Zone

Pavilion : Nordic Pavilion

Note : The general theme of the exhibition is "Oasis in the North." It is a joint pavilion of the five Nordic countries, i.e., Denmark, Finland, Iceland, Norway and Sweden, which share similar natural surroundings, histories and languages etc.

001

001-003

Zone : Europe Zone
Pavilion : Nordic Pavilion
Item : The Entrance of the Pavilion
Note : On the wall near the entrance, there are five screens offering information about respective features of the five countries.

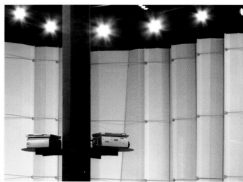

002

003

004-006

Zone : Europe Zone
Pavilion : Nordic Pavilion
Item : The Interior
Note : Inside the pavilion there is the Nordic Loop made of fir from Finland, which is thus shrouded in the sweet smell of trees. From opposite the Nordic Loop, visitors can see images of the waterfall. The walls of the main exhibition hall are covered by snow-white wallpaper. Through videos, photos, costumes, and tools etc, visitors can catch a glimpse of Nordic lifestyle, which is close to nature, easy and relaxing.

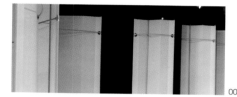

004

005

006

The Americas Zone

United States of America
Canada
Mexico
United Nations
Central America Pavilion

001-021

Zone : The Americas Zone

Pavilion : United States of America

Note : The theme of the U.S. Pavilion is "The Franklin Spirit." It introduces American people's respect for nature from a unique perspective.

001

002

003

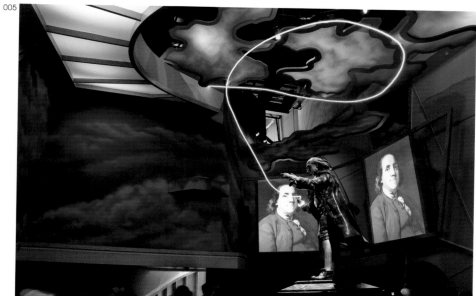

004-006

Zone : The Americas Zone

Pavilion : United States of America

Item : Exhibition

Note : With the illuminated Franklin's kite overhead, visitors are led into the main show that is hosted by Benjamin Franklin. Under his guidance, visitors look back at the research on nature and its amazing potentials in the last 300 years, and also get more information about today's America and its attitude towards nature.

007

008

007-009

Zone : The Americas Zone
Pavilion : United States of America
Item : The Theatre
Note : The three-dimensional image of Benjamin Franklin will appear in the theatre, and he will give an account of the development of American nature, science and technology during the recent 200 years. The shocking audiovisual effects bring about vivid feelings.

009

010

011

012

013

010-021

Zone : The Americas Zone

Pavilion : United States of America

Item : The American Journey Gallery

Note : The American Journey gallery in the U.S. Pavilion exhibits marking milestones on a journey of progress and innovation. Among the exhibits in the gallery is a true-to-life replica of the 1902 Wright Glider created by Orville and Wilbur Wright as they developed the first airplane. Other exhibits include displays of fascinating new images received daily from missions to Mars and Saturn, a Fuel Cell exhibit that explores a solution for meeting future energy demands, and a vision of future automotive technology presented by General Motors.

017

018

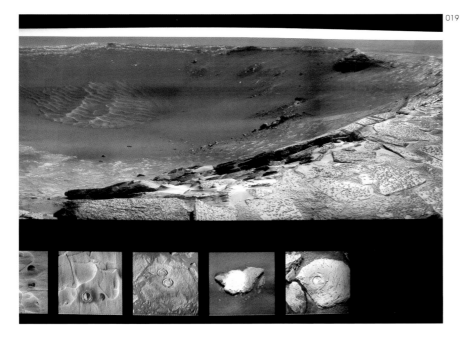

019

020

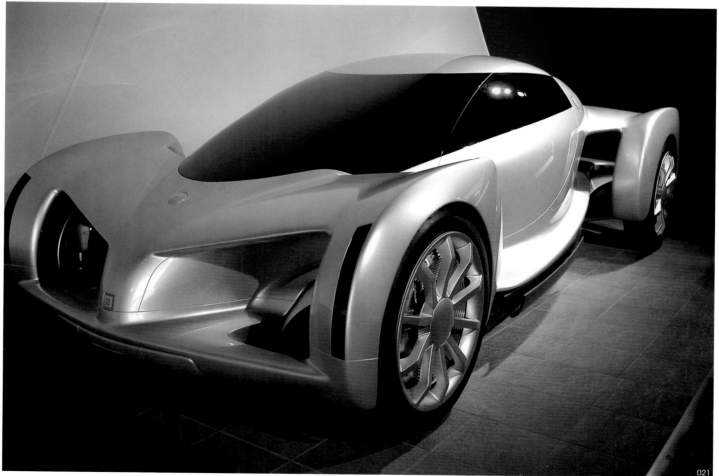

021

001-010

Zone : The Americas Zone

Pavilion : Canada

Note : The theme of the Canada Pavilion is "Wisdom of Diversity." Through vivid multi-media presentations, visitors are acquainted with magnificent Canadian forests, seas and prairies, and its ethnic diversity.

004

005

006

007

004·010

Zone : The Americas Zone

Pavilion : Canada

Item : The Interior

Note : In the pavilion, the multi-layered wire webs on the walls function as screens and together with the video screens on the walls make up a multi-layered experiential theatre. Visitors can enjoy Canadian natural beauty and cultural diversity to their hearts' content here.

001-020

Zone : The Americas Zone
Pavilion : Mexico
Note : The exhibits at the pavilion are shown under the theme "Complicatedly Intertwined Diversity: Changing Nature and Culture" against the background of Mexico's unique culture and the national land rich in changes.

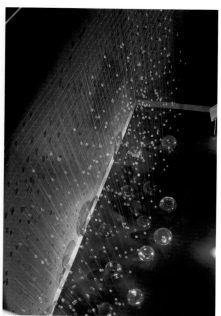

004

Zone : The Americas Zone
Pavilion : Mexico
Item : The Steam Screen
Note : You need to pass the translucent steam screen that shows images of aquatic biodiversity to enter the pavilion.

005-006

Zone : The Americas Zone
Pavilion : Mexico
Item : The Interior
Note : Entering the pavilion, visitors will be delighted to see on the pool the 15 ball-shaped water-filled glasses with a diameter of 25cm, and many other water-filled glass balls above, which are crystal and shining.

007-019

Zone : The Americas Zone

Pavilion : Mexico

Item : The Exhibition Hall

Note : At the exhibition hall, visitors can experience four chief ecosystems - sea, desert, forest and jungle - via videos and other visual images. Traditional artifacts, modern art works and ancient collections are also shown.

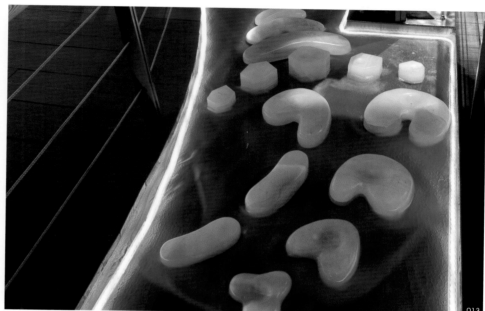

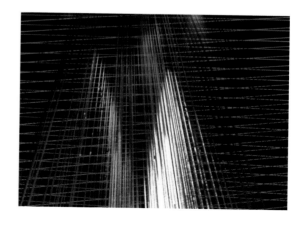

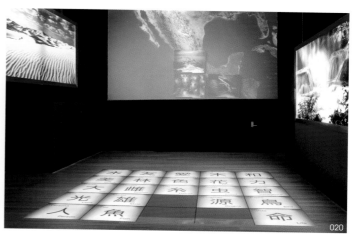

020

Zone : The Americas Zone

Pavilion : Mexico

Item : Interactive Installation

Note : When visitors enter a certain area, the screen on the wall will immediately inform them of relevant contents.

001-003

Zone : The Americas Zone

Pavilion : United Nations

Note : With the theme of "Celebrating Diversity", more than 30 U.N. organizations have gathered at the pavilion. These diversities include those of life, cultures, peoples, states and the United Nations' own work. Through the work of the U.N. families, the U.N. Pavilion portrays the people across the world and praises their diversity. Things worth seeing are impressionistic video art exhibits, photos entered in an international competition sponsored by the U.N. Environment Program (UNEP), and the "Art Gallery" showing exhibits about aging and health problems.

002

003

001-007

Zone : The Americas Zone

Pavilion : Central America Pavilion

Note : Central America is an area facing both the Pacific and Atlantic oceans. The differences of the two oceans are shown in beautiful submarine images and in an exhibition of rare sand. At the same time, the Panama Canal linking the two oceans is introduced.

001

002

003

002-003

Zone : The Americas Zone

Pavilion : Central America Pavilion

Item : Exhibits

Note : Various tropical rainforests are reproduced using genuine plants. Various animals, insects and birds in Central America are also shown on a large screen.

004-007

Zone : The Americas Zone
Pavilion : Central America Pavilion
Item : Exhibitions
Note : The differences of the two oceans are shown in beautiful submarine images and in an exhibition of rare sand. At the same time, the Panama Canal linking the two oceans is introduced.In addition, the wisdom and techniques of people in the ancient times are introduced by visual images and exhibitions of various civilizations, such as Mayan, Toltec and Olmec. Also shown is the fact that coffee is playing an important role in the preservation of forests.

007

Oceania and
Southeast Asia Zone

Australia
Philippines
Cambodia
Malaysia
Singapore
New Zealand
Indonesia
Thailand

001-008

Zone : Oceania and Southeast Asia Zone
Pavilion : Australia
Note : The theme of Australian pavilion is "We have to protect and preserve our environment for future generations." The pavilion takes visitors on a journey through time, starting back 65,000 years ago, when indigenous people lived in complete harmony with the land.

001

002

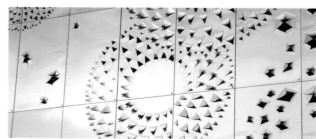

001

Zone : Oceania and Southeast Asia Zone
Pavilion : Australia
Item : External Design
Note : The facade is designed by studio 505 and Geoff Nees and makes use of stainless steel and takes its inspiration from the Southern Cross, one of Australia's best know constellations.

003-006

Zone : Oceania and Southeast Asia Zone

Pavilion : Australia

Item : Data Forest

Note : Some 80 plasma screens form "data totems" rising from the floor of the pavilion – a fascinating combination of Australia's indigenous past and technologically advanced present. The data totems tell a story of a modern, culturally diverse and harmonious nation with a successful economy – today's Australian experience.

007-008

Zone : Oceania and Southeast Asia Zone

Pavilion : Australia

Item : Internal Exhibition Hall

Note : In this room, visitors meet the star of the Australian pavilion, an 11-meter-long model of a platypus on a riverbank. The platypus was chosen because it existed 65,000 years ago and has remained largely unchanged since that time. The message here is to provide the environment for safe and sustainable development in the future.

001-010

Zone : Oceania and Southeast Asia Zone

Pavilion : Philippines

Note : The Philippines pavilion's theme is "Usbong: Seeds of Life." It showcases a variety of coconut-based exhibits because the Philippines is one of the world's largest exporter of coconuts. The exterior of the dome-shaped pavilion, made up of bits of fabrics, looks like a cross-section of a coconut. Indigenous habitants' poems are carved onto the fabrics.

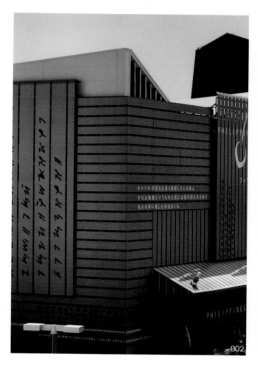

005

005-007

Zone : Oceania and Southeast Asia Zone

Pavilion : Philippines

Item : The Interior

Note : Stepping inside, visitors stand on modernly engineered coconut floors. The walls and ceiling are continuous weaving using panels of Philippine fabrics and textiles of "silk cocoon" woven to architectural specifications. The walls double as screens in themselves. Most interesting is a 7-meter-diameter sphere, called "Essences," a cocoon of "Health and Wellness."

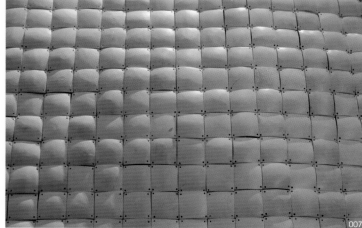

008

Zone : Oceania and Southeast Asia Zone

Pavilion : Philippines

Item : The Restaurant

Note : The façade of the restaurant in the pavilion is uniquely made of rattan whips.

009-010

Zone : Oceania and Southeast Asia Zone

Pavilion : Philippines

Item : "Essences"

Note : Entering the spherical exhibition hall "Essences", visitors will find that the walls and seats in this huge "coconut" are made of jute packing, so they are very soft.

001-004

Zone : Oceania and Southeast Asia Zone
Pavilion : Cambodia
Note : Cambodia's participation in EXPO 2005 reflects its desire to get its rich cultural heritage and potential economic development to be better understood by people around the world. Another aim is to showcase close links between the Cambodian people and nature, such as its jungles and big lakes.

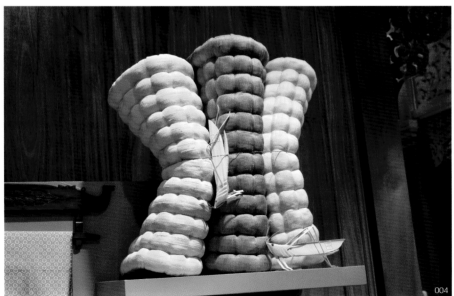

002-004

Zone : Oceania and Southeast Asia Zone
Pavilion : Cambodia
Item : Exhibition
Note : Traditional complex silk weaving is demonstrated throughout the six-month Expo period, along with several arts performances, including stone carving. Visitors will likely be charmed by the techniques that were used to build and carve the Angkor Wat temples 1,000 years ago.

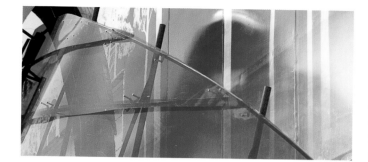

001-005

Zone : Oceania and Southeast Asia Zone

Pavilion : Malaysia

Note : The theme of the Malaysian pavilion is "Truly Natural. Infinitely Harmonious." Malaysia is characterized as a multiracial and multicultural country and is home to some of the world's oldest rainforests. With these facts in mind, the pavilion showcases the grand landscape of rainforests and images of beautiful coral reefs.

001

002

001-005

Zone : Oceania and Southeast Asia Zone
Pavilion : Malaysia
Item : Four Corners
Note : The Malaysian pavilion is divided into four corners: "Song of the Rainforest" to introduce varied species of plants and animals, "Chorus of Life" to present the Putrajaya Wetland, the largest manmade wetland in the tropics, "Rhythms of Celebration" that is the collection of an array of cultural and religious festivals, and "Symphony of Green" aimed at developing cities in harmony with nature.

001-016

Zone : Oceania and Southeast Asia Zone

Pavilion : Singapore

Note : The Singaporean pavilion showcases "Blending of City Environment and Garden City, Harmony of the Past and the Present, and Work and Leisure, and Interfusion of a Variety of Cultures."

003-006

Zone : Oceania and Southeast Asia Zone
Pavilion : Singapore
Item : "Nature of City"
Note : The rainy "Nature of City" area on the grass provides visitors with an opportunity to see the great strides Singapore has made in afforestation despite the country being a city-state. At the entrance, the smiling staff will give each visitor a transparent umbrella. The indoor tropical flora park is refreshing. Through the effects of lighting, sound, rainfall and videos, visitors will experience tropical forests by themselves. Rain falls on the umbrella, the stream gurgles, and the fragrance of flowers fills the air. In the drizzle, visitors get to know via the giant screen this modern city with both natural beauty and diversified cultures, and how it has realized harmony between different cultures and between man and nature.

007-009

Zone : Oceania and Southeast Asia Zone
Pavilion : Singapore
Item : Internal Design
Note : This is the corridor of light and video images.

007

008

009

010-014

Zone : Oceania and Southeast Asia Zone
Pavilion : Singapore
Item : Internal Design

014

015

016

015-016
Zone : Oceania and Southeast Asia Zone
Pavilion : Singapore
Item : "Memory Coming Down to Future Generations" Library
Note : The "Memory Coming Down to Future Generations" area is a library where visitors can read books of reminiscences based on firsthand experiences of Singapore people.

001-006

Zone : Oceania and Southeast Asia Zone
Pavilion : New Zealand
Note : The New Zealand pavilion is a firsthand experience-type pavilion which showcases four themes - New, Sea, Land and People - using a variety of imaging techniques.

001-002

Zone : Oceania and Southeast Asia Zone
Pavilion : New Zealand
Item : External Design
Note : The exterior of the pavilion is dominated by a man-made white cloud, visually representing both New Zealand/Aotearoa (which translated means "the land of the long white cloud") and the water cycle which sustains its rich natural resources.

002

003

004-006

Zone : Oceania and Southeast Asia Zone

Pavilion : New Zealand

Item : Exhibition

Note : The cloud floats into the interior of the pavilion, where a wide-screen multiple projection film greets visitors with the sight of a bird's flight across New Zealand's landscape. The cloud condenses and falls onto a 1.8 tonne greenstone (pounamu) boulder from the bed of the Waitaiki creek, by the Arahura River on the West Coast. As visitors touch the stone they will be touching the "heart" of New Zealand .

004

005

006

001-004

Zone : Oceania and Southeast Asia Zone

Pavilion : Indonesia

Note : As its theme, the Indonesia Pavilion has "Integrating People and Nature: Building Eco-Community in Harmony". Visitors see the world of Indonesia under water in the sea and fresh water aquariums. They are directed through the Biodiversity Corridor under the jungle canopy with sounds and images of the Indonesian jungle presented through multimedia devices.

001

002

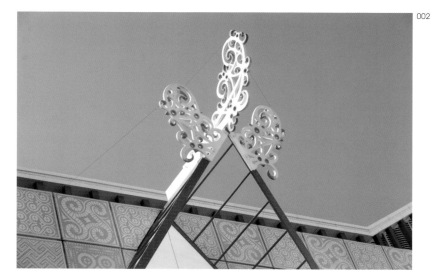

003

004

001-004

Zone : Oceania and Southeast Asia Zone

Pavilion : Thailand

Note : The Thai pavilion showcases landscapes and lives of Thai people in various parts of the country and a variety of their customs, particularly wisdom of Thai people. Hence, the theme of the Thai exhibition is "Art of Life."

001

002

001-008

Zone : Africa Zone
Pavilion : Egypt
Note : The theme of the Egyptian Pavilion is "Eternal Egypt." As the point of contact for the three continents of Asia, Africa and Europe, Egypt has built a unique national identity through a process of interaction with various civilizations and cultures.

005-008

Zone : Africa Zone
Pavilion : Egypt
Item : Exhibits
Note : From the ages of the ancient pharaohs and their glories to modern Egypt, the exhibition presents a graphical synopsis of the country's culture and history, as well as major tourist attractions. Replica statues of the pharaohs are also on display.

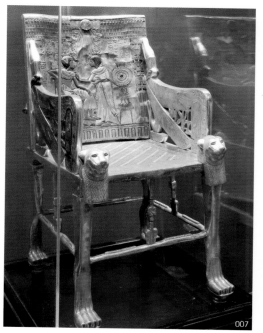

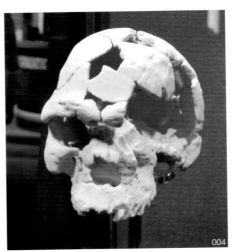

001-016

Zone : Africa Zone

Pavilion : The Joint African Pavilion

Note : The joint African pavilion consists of exhibitions provided by 28 African countries, and exhibits are displayed, from north to south, according to the geographical location of the host countries. Visitors can view virtually the entire African continent as if taking a real tour of the countries concerned. Under the general theme "The Great Ballad of Africa," the exhibitions present colorful attractions of various African countries.

005

006

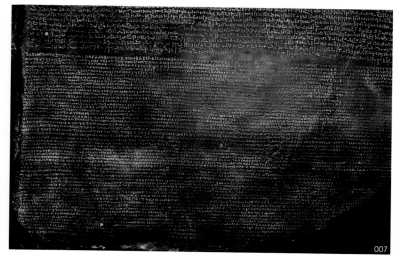

007

001-012

Zone : Africa Zone

Pavilion : The Joint African Pavilion

Item : Exhibition Areas

Note : The exhibition areas of the participating countries are filled with exhibits that symbolize their rich cultures and traditions. The art gallery contains native masks, tableware, clothing and other objects that portray the African history and traditions. The facade of the pavilion features wall paintings on African sceneries, enhancing the African mood of the exhibitions.

008

014

015

016

EXPO PLAZA

001-008

Zone : Central Zone

Pavilion : EXPO Plaza

Note : On the green EXPO Plaza you will experience communication and exchange events that symbolize a Grand Intercultural Symphony. With the adoption of the latest technology in communications and digital videoing, visitors and people around the world can get in contact.

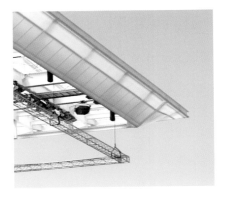

001

002

003

001-008

Zone: Central Zone
Pavilion: EXPO Plaza
Item: Environment and Facilities
Note: The lawn in the middle of the EXPO Plaza can hold around 3,000 visitors. Right in front of Expo Plaza stands Bio Lung, a vertical wall filled with flowers and plants. Behind the Bio Lung is the large videoing installation "EXPO Vision", which is the biggest outdoor screen in Japan, 840 inches. EXPO Vision shows all sorts of image contents as well as footage taken with cameras at EXPO 2005 events. World famous performers also make their appearance here.

007

008

001-004

Zone : Central Zone

Pavilion : In the Evening at Koi Pond

Note : The Koi Pond is at the center of EXPO site, next to the Global House. It is
a tranquil pond filled with multicolored carp. Each night at 8 p.m. for about
30 minutes, the Koi Pond itself becomes a major attraction as the scene for
an experimental theater event featuring the interaction between nature and
humans. It is Choreographed with impact and beauty by world-renowned artist
Robert Wilson, "a towering figure in the world of experimental theater."

001

001

Zone : Central Zone

Pavilion : In the Evening at Koi Pond

Item : Model of the Japanese Monkey

Note : In the middle of Koi Pond is a giant model of a
Japanese monkey, which can turning around, blinking
eyes and twist its mouth.

002

003

004

002-004

Zone : Central Zone

Pavilion : In the Evening at Koi Pond

Item : The Performance

Note : The background setting of the performance is the dark wood beside the pond. The fountain produces a large water screen. The reflection of the fluorescence of the screen on water surface adorns the pond with splendid colors. Then gradually the main role of the performance ---- a Japanese monkey ascends from the depth of the pond. It is the messenger from forests, conveying to human race the wisdom of nature. The performance has four parts: Earth, Life, Civilization and Future. The audience experiences a memorable journey of the eye.

001-007

Zone : Central Zone
Pavilion : Global House
Note : Global House, a project planned by the Association, is designed to let visitors experience "Nature's Wisdom" firsthand and look ahead for future global society. The remains of the extinct mammoth from Siberia are on show here.

001

Zone : Central Zone
Pavilion : Global House
Item : Its Emblem
Note : The blue sphere of the emblem represents the shape of the Earth, the crystallization of "Nature's Wisdom," and the orange sphere represents "creativity and vitality." The emblem was chosen as a symbol of the hope that one day, their coexistence will be possible.

002-007

Zone : Central Zone

Pavilion : Global House

Item : Exterior of the Construction

Note : Global House takes the shape of the two facilities it originally accommodated - an ice skating rink and a heated pool. The west wing is called "Blue Hall" and the east wing "Orange Hall" in recognition of the emblem's colors and for ease in guiding visitors and transmitting the theme. The Mammoth Laboratory, which houses the frozen remains of the Yukagir Mammoth, can be viewed from both wings.

BIO-LUNG

001-005

Zone: Central Zone

Pavilion: Bio-lung

Note: At the center of EXPO Plaza is the Bio Lung, an experimental vertical wall filled with flowers and plants. Bio Lung was made for the purpose of improving the environment of busy city areas where enormous amount of CO₂ is emitted which causes the serious problem such as global warming phenomenon and heat island phenomenon.

001

002

001-003

Zone: Central Zone

Pavilion: Bio-lung

Item: The Vertical Green Wall

Note: Bio Lung is a vertical wall filled with flowers and plants. With a height ranging from 4.5 to 15 meters, a length of 150 meters, and 3,500 m2 area. More than 200 kind of plants and flowers are planted in this great wall and there are more than 200 thousands pots.

003

004

005

004-005

Zone : Central Zone

Pavilion : Bio-lung

Item : The Building Structure

Note : The Bio Lung is built on re-usable steel-reinforced base structures. Different types of 1350mm multi-purpose green panel modules can be attached to these 1500mm grid base structures. This type of independent building structure is designed to be able to function in any kind of urban environment, and incorporates a 'backyard' area, which can be used for maintenance.

001-006

Zone : Central Zone

Pavilion : Friendship Center

Note : Friendship Center is set up in memory of the 100th anniversary of the Rotary Club.

Paul Percy Harris founded the Rotary Club in 1905, which holds the principles of mutual friendship and international fraternity. Outside the pavilion, the pool and trees are refreshing; inside it there is exhibition in honor of the 100th anniversary of Rotary Club and the conference room.

004

005

006

Environment & Facilities

Services
Public Art
Gardens
Visual Information
Transport

001-026

Item : Environment & Facilities

Note : The EXPO site receives hundreds of thousands of visitors every day. The sponsor has placed emphasis on the construction of facilities such as restaurants and stores etc so that visitors can enjoy the wonders of this exposition to the full.

001

002

001-002

Item : U.S. Bistro Route 66

003-004
Item : Victoria Barbecue Garden

005
Item : Rstrante Dolce Italia

006

007

006-007

Item : Japanese Restaurant NADAMAN

008-010

Item : ASAHI PANORAMA RESTRAURANT

008

009

010

011

012

011-012

Item : Restaurants in Japan Zone

014

Item : Curry Shop CHITAKA

015-016
Item : The Vending-machine

017
Item : Official Cart

018

Item : Public Repose Area

019-020

Item : The Stand of Koi Pond

021

Item : Washing Room in Linear Car Station

021

022

023

024

022-024

Item : Chairs on Global Loop

025

026

001-022
Item : Public Art
Note : The EXPO site has a strong artistic atmosphere. There are various artistic activities. Many young artists are also invited to present their works in the exposition. Visitors come across varied works of public art in all the zones.

001

002

003

001-003
Item : Player Alien
Note : Player Alien is a 6 meter-tall gigantic sculpture made of multiple parts. Looking at a distance with some parts missing, the artwork projects a message that life is precious because each of us is different and incomplete. It leads you to the "search of happiness". Artist:Risa Sato (Japan), born in 1972 in Tokyo.

004

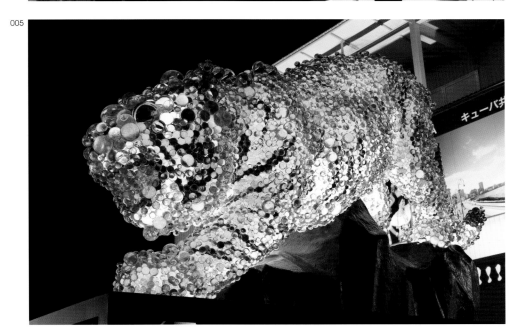

005

001-010

Item : The Art Program

Note : The Art Program, which is the official event of EXPO 2005, introduces works by young artists representing today's world and serves a bridge to the innovative culture of the 21st century. The artists, who were born after 1970 and grew up in a new era where existing values and ethics have dramatically shifted, present their ideas in a form of sculpture and photography in seven different locations within the EXPO grounds.

006

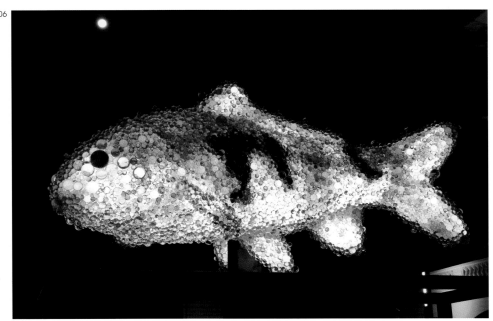

004-006

Item : PixCell-Sacred Beast

Note : A fierce tiger and a swelling carp, both having a sacred image and story, are covered with transparent beads. The artworks symbolize the dialogue between modern-day humans and animals historically depicted with significant meanings.

Artist: Kohei Nawa (Japan), born in 1975 in Osaka.

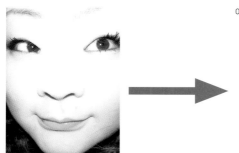

007·008

Item：FACE

Note：Her work consists of a gigantic portrait of herself disguising as 12 different people, suitable to this international environment. It addresses the importance of love-sharing and co-existing among all human beings, regardless of nationality or ethnicity.

Artist: Tomoko Sawada (Japan), born in1977 in Hyogo Prefecture.

009

Item : Guardian Angels

Note : Large-sized dwarf fairies modeled after a mascot Europeans commonly display in their yards. The fairies keep their eyes on us humans and the nature as we all gather around at the square. Artist: Ivana Falconi, born in 1970in Locarno, Switzerland

010

Item : World Map

Note : This work consists of 4 paintings of bright colored World Map, changing the size, shape and location of countries, on the floor of a pond that brings visitors in direct contact with water. The work addresses the relationship and issues between "water and countries". Artist: Federico Hererro,born in 1978 Costa Rica.

011

Item : Washing Basins

Note : The basins installed at the outdoor public areas are distinctive porcelain works, created by Japanese experts in porcelain art.

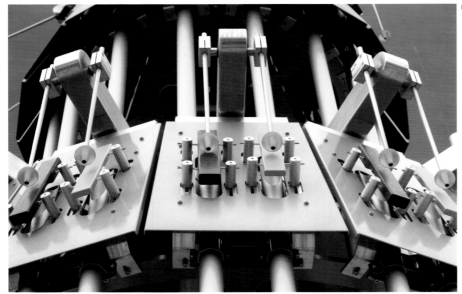

012-014

Item : Instruments of Wind

Note : Around the Earth Tower are implements that convert the wind into sound. The sound varies with the change of wind. Visitors are immersed in the harmony of nature.

015

Item: The Gigantic Umbrella

Note: This is the Gigantic Umbrella located in the middle of the plaza in European and Mederterranian Zone. It is foldable. It shields visitors from sunshine and rainfall, and forms an attractive scene.

016

Item: Decorative Road Lamps

Note: The road lamps in in European and Mederterranian Zone are impressive with giant glass covers.

016

017

Item: Japanese Tower—The Moon

Note: The exterior of Japanese Tower—The Moon in Japan Zone combines the images of the moon and a dashing ship etc. It expresses the mystery of life, respect for nature and the steps of human civilization.

017

018-019

Item : Sculptures Turning in Wind
Note : The sculptures by the sides of Global Loop and in the central plaza turn around gracefully with the wind.

020

Item : Evening Scenery
Note : This picture shows evening sights around the Koi Pond.

001-018

Item : Gardening

Note : The EXPO site is located in an undulating hilly area with magnificent natural beauty. To embody the concept of environment protection, natural surroundings have been preserved to the largest extent despite the building of all these pavilions. Various gardens connect different zones. The pavilions are all decorated with trees and flowers.

004

001-006

Item : Gardening
Note : This garden is situated between Japan Zone and Central Zone. It is ornamented with bright flowers. The most attractive are the dotted glass flowers.

005

006

007-009
Item : Gardening
Note : The Morizo tree and Kiccoro tree are greeting visitors.

010-011

Item : Gardening

Note : Flowers in the basket hanging on the wall are so thriving. The planting method is superb.

010

011

012

013

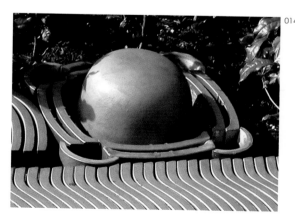

014

012-014

Item : Gardening

Note : This kind of special tiles can be used to build pavilions and decorate gardens, giving them a Japanese touch.

015-017

Item : Gardening

Note : EXPO Aichi can be called an exposition of flora with a variety of flowers. Japanese gardening impresses visitors.

001-026

Item : Visual Direction

Note : To bring convenience to visitors, a complete visual direction system is indispensable. EXPO Aichi is a good example in this regard.

001

Item : The Symbol Pavilion

003

Item : "EXPO 2005 Aichi, Japan" Advertisement and Mascot

001

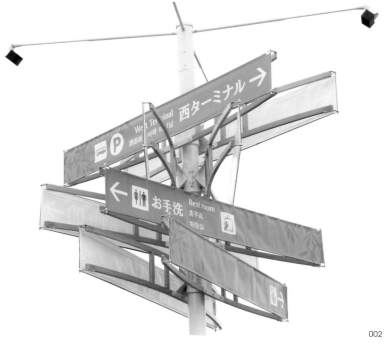

002

003

004

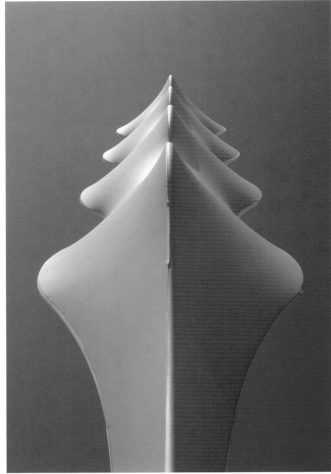

005

006

004-006

Item : Corporate Pavilion Zone Sign Pole

007-008
Item : Asia Zone Sign Pole

009
Item : Oceania and Southeast Asia Zone Sign Pole

010
Item : Africa Zone Sign Pole

011
Item : The Americas Zone Sign Pole

013

012
Item : Europe and Mediterranean Zone Sign Pole

014

013
Item : Europe and Mediterranean Zone Lamp

015

016

014
Item : Europe Zone Sign Pole

017-020

Item : The Plan

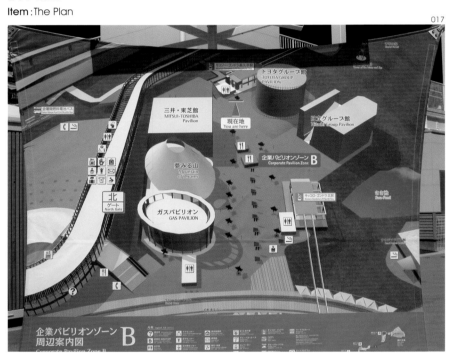

021-025
Item : Route Signpost
026
Item : Signpost

001-011

Item : Transportation

Note : World Expositions are the longest and the liveliest international pageants. Transportation is critical for the holding of a successful exposition. In accordance with its theme and environmental protection concept, transportation tools in EXPO Aichi site are all environmentally friendly. The most advanced technology nowadays and the trend of future vehicles are also introduced.

001

001

Item : Global Loop

Note : Global Loop, a huge elevated circular walkway, is designed to require minimal modification to the area's topography and is erected so as to detour around existing natural ponds and precious habitats of fauna and flora. The Global Loop leads visitors to six Global Commons and Corporate Pavilions. This 2.6 km-long walkway has three sections: a middle section made of a 50%-by-50% mixture of waste wood and waste plastic, and two side sections made of Brazilian eucalyptus. It takes over 1 hour for visitors to walk around it.

002

002

Item : Kiccoro Gondola/Morizo Gondola

Note : Kiccoro Gondola facilitates transportation between north and south of Nagakute site, while Morizo Gondola and fuel cell hybrid buses are used to connect Nagakute site and Seto site. The gonbola passes by many civil houses, so its glass wndows become opaque when it gets close to the houses, in order to protect privacy of those residents. When it is away from the houses, the windows will become transparent again.

003

Item : Linimo

Note : "Linimo" refers to the linear motor car, whose highest speed reaches 100km per hour. It has three carriages holding in total 244 passengers. It is Japan's first maglev train service operating between Yakusa and Fujigaoka Stations to Nagakute Station located next to the EXPO 2005 site.

004

Item : IMTS

Note : IMTS (Intelligent Multimode Transit System) applies the latest intelligent transport system (ITS) technology. The unmanned, automatic IMTS vehicles are mounted with engines fueled with clean compressed natural gas (CNG) and steered and controlled by magnetic markers imbedded in the middle of the dedicated road. Its maximum speed is 30 kilometers per hour.

005

Item : Inter-Venue Fuel Cell Bus

Note : The inter-venue fuel cell bus operates on motors powered by high-pressure hydrogen-supplied fuel cells and a nickel-metal hydride secondary battery. It does not emit carbon dioxide or other toxic substances during operation. Instead it emits only water.

006

Item : Global Tram

Note : The Global Tram is a pleasant mode of transportation that is battery-powered and operates over the Global Loop. Each tram is composed of three cars: a driving car and 2 passenger cars, holding 52 passengers and 2 wheelchairs. Its speed is 5km per hour.

007-008

Item : Small-sized Car Used by EXPO Staff

009-010

Item : Bicycle Taxicabs (Velo taxis)

Note : Bicycle taxicabs (Velo taxis) are jointly developed by three Japanese corporarions. It is easy to ride with the application of advanced technology. Even elders can ride it. It is especially good for your health to ride this kind of Velo taxi. Moreover, its environmentally friendly design is in line with the theme of "Love the Earth".

011

Item : Mini-bus for Tour and Performance

001-012

Item : EXPO Hall

Note : EXPO Hall is used for theme conferences and activities.

005

004-005

Item : EXPO Dome

Note : During the exposition, artists from around the world give performances in EXPO Dome, which can hold 3,000 audiences.

007

Item : The Canopy of Global Loop

008-009

Item : Satellite Studio

010
Item : Plaza and Architecture at the North Gate

011
Item : Satellite Studio

012
Item : Architecture and the Souvenir Store

001-020

Zone : Forest Experience Zone
Note : This zone makes full use of thriving plants in the Youth Park.
A lot of new trees have also been cultivated. Visitors marvel at
exceptional Japanese gardens in this zone.

001-003

Zone : Forest Experience Zone
Item : Satsuki and Mei's House
Note : A replica of the Kusakabe residence, a house of the 1950s in which
the lead characters of Studio Ghibi's 1988 animated feature "My Neighbor
Totoro" lived, has been built within the woods of the Expo site. It has been
constructed using techniques of the early Showa era and undergone
artificial aging. The furnishings have also beween made to reflect the
movie as faithfully as possible.

004

005

006

007

008

009

010

004-016

Zone : Forest Experience Zone

Item : Japanese Garden

Note : The garden enables visitors to observe different aspects and facets of water, making use of Kaede pond, Medaka pond and other geographical and water features. By comparing variations of the landscape along the river running east-west to the passage of time in the manufacturing process from stone and soil to pottery, this new approach to garden design symbolizes the climate and culture of Aichi based on the craftsmanship from past to present.

Interactive Fun Zone

Family Ai-land & Tokimeki Museum
Growing Village
NGO Global Village
Wind Square
Water Square
Robot Station

001-018

Zone : Interactive Fun Zone
Pavilion : Family Ai-land & Tokimeki Ai-land
Item : Tokimeki Island

004-006

Zone : Interactive Fun Zone

Pavilion : Family Ai-land & Tokimeki Ai-land

Item : Disk-O Thrill Ride

Note : The Tokimeki Ai-land amusement park has the first Disk-O thrill ride in Japan and a haunted house, offering amusement for families.

004

005

006

009

Zone : Interactive Fun Zone
Pavilion : Family Ai-land & Tokimeki Ai-land
Item : The Haunted House

010

009

011

010-011

Zone : Interactive Fun Zone
Pavilion : Family Ai-land & Tokimeki Ai-land
Item : Play Facilities

012

012-014
Zone : Interactive Fun Zone
Pavilion : Family Ai-land & Tokimeki Ai-land
Item : Play Facilities

013

014

015
Zone : Interactive Fun Zone
Pavilion : Family Ai-land & Tokimeki Ai-land
Item : The Windmill Park

016-017
Zone : Interactive Fun Zone
Pavilion : Family Ai-land & Tokimeki Ai-land
Item : Ferris wheel
Note : The 88-meter-high Ferris wheel is the tallest in the Tokai region. The Ferris wheel with 6-passenger cabins in the Family Ai-land completes its turn in 13 minutes, enabling one to enjoy a full view of the site. Other play facilities are also available.

001-015

Zone : Interactive Fun Zone

Pavilion : Growing Village

004

005

006

007

008

009

001-015

Zone : Interactive Fun Zone

Pavilion : Growing Village

Note : Trees can teach us a lot of things. In the Growing Village, there are wooden houses and plank ways dotted in the forests. Visitors climb trees and participate in other activities in the wooden house. In this way, they experience nature and marvel at the mystery of life.

LAUGHING HAPPY TREE PARK
木笑園

In the spring of 2000 John Gathright and the Laughing Park Team won the prestigious JIDPO Good Design Award for Ecology Design. A portion of the original Laughing Tree Park has been replanted in the Laughing Tree Park at the Growing Village.

2000年春から、ジョン・ギャスライトの考えに賛同した仲間たちが育てている「木笑園」（2000年エコロジーデザイン部門グッドデザイン賞受賞）。その一部がグローイングヴィレッジに移植されています。

Artist　**JOHN GATHRIGHT**
作者　**& Laughing Tree Park Team**
　　　ジョン ギャスライトと木笑園チーム
　　　Seto　瀬戸市

013

014

015

001

002

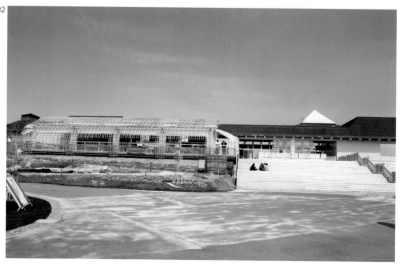

001-008

Zone : Interactive Fun Zone

Pavilion : NGO Global Village

Note : NGO Global Village is situated in the nothwest of Nagakute site. It consists of the indoor Meeting Zone and the outdoor Experience and Exchange Zone.

001-006

Zone : Interactive Fun Zone
Pavilion : NGO Global Village
Item : Meeting Zone
Note : The Meeting Zone provides information on the meaning and concept of a global village, and the partnership of the sponsor enterprises.

003

004

005

006

007

008

007-008

Zone : Interactive Fun Zone
Pavilion : NGO Global Village
Item : Experience and Exchange Zone
Note : There are five exhibition rooms made of bamboo where display and experiential discussion are held, and a multi-functional hall. The rooms and the hall are all egg-shaped, made of natural materials such as bamboo, wood, soil and cloth etc. The whole construction is in perfect harmony with its surroundings.

001-019

Zone : Interactive Fun Zone

Pavilion : The Wind Square & the Water Square

Note : To the north of the Global Loop is located a 1500 square
meters plaza whose theme is "Flowers, Water, Wind and the Sun".
This plaza is made up of Wind Square and Water Square.

001

002

003

004

001-007

Zone : Interactive Fun Zone

Pavilion : Wind Square

Note : The focus of this square is of course wind. Windmills can be seen everywhere. Its trails paved with woodchips are friendly to your feet.

WATER SQUARE

008-015

Zone : Interactive Fun Zone

Item : The Water Square

Originality : Water Square is a wonderful place where flowers vie for attention, and the fountain with solar power devices brings coolness to visitors. One can walk around comfortably or enjoy swimming and other programs with water

011

012

013

014

015

016

017

018

019

016-019

Zone : Interactive Fun Zone
Item : The Water Square
Note : Water is the source of life. In this Water Square, visitors are led to focus on water. In mid-summer, water brings coolness and a lot of fun.

ROBOT STATION

001-002

Zone : Interactive Fun Zone
Item : Robot Station
Note : The Robot Station is a venue for demonstrations by working robots, a place for interaction between visitors and robots, and a base for the maintenance of the working robots.

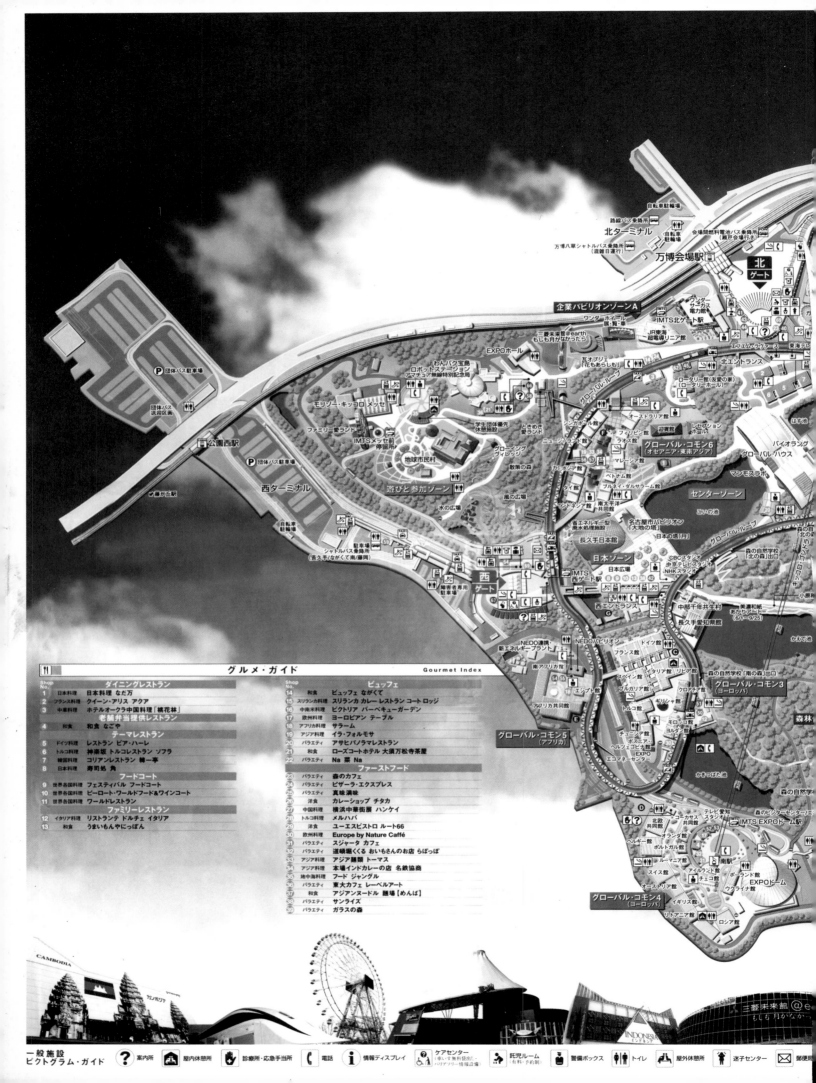

グルメ・ガイド — Gourmet Index

Shop No.		
ダイニングレストラン		
1	日本料理	日本料理 なだ万
2	フランス料理	クイーン・アリス アクア
3	中華料理	ホテルオークラ中国料理「桃花林」
老舗弁当提供レストラン		
4	和食	和食 なごや
テーマレストラン		
5	ドイツ料理	レストラン ビア・ハーレ
6	トルコ料理	神楽坂 トルコレストラン ソフラ
7	韓国料理	コリアンレストラン 緒一亭
8	日本料理	寿司処 角
フードコート		
9	世界各国料理	フェスティバル フードコート
10	世界各国料理	ビーロート・ワールドフード&ワインコート
11	世界各国料理	ワールドレストラン
ファミリーレストラン		
12	イタリア料理	リストランテ ドルチェ イタリア
13	和食	うまいもんやにっぽん

Shop No.		
ビュッフェ		
14	和食	ビュッフェ ながくて
15	スリランカ料理	スリランカ カレー レストラン コート ロッジ
16	中南米料理	ビクトリア バーベキューガーデン
17	欧州料理	ヨーロピアン テーブル
18	アフリカ料理	サラーム
19	アジア料理	イラ・フォルモサ
20	バラエティ	アサヒパノラマレストラン
21	和食	ローズコートホテル 大須万松寺茶屋
22	バラエティ	Na 菜 Na
ファーストフード		
23	バラエティ	森のカフェ
24	バラエティ	ピザーラ・エクスプレス
25	バラエティ	真味満味
26	洋食	カレーショップ チタカ
27	中国料理	横浜中華街展 ハンケイ
28	トルコ料理	メルハバ
29	洋食	ユーエスビストロ ルート66
30	欧州料理	Europe by Nature Caffé
31	バラエティ	スジャータ カフェ
32	バラエティ	道頓堀くくる おいもさんのお店 らぽっぽ
33	アジア料理	アジア麺類 トーマス
34	アジア料理	本場インドカレーの店 名鉄協商
45	地中海料理	フード ジャングル
36	東大カフェ	レーベルアート
37	和食	アジアンヌードル 麺場【めんば】
38	バラエティ	サンライズ
39	バラエティ	ガラスの森

一般施設 ピクトグラム・ガイド

? 案内所　屋内休憩所　診療所・応急手当所　電話　情報ディスプレイ　ケアセンター（車いす無料貸出し・バリアフリー情報設備）　託児ルーム（有料・予約制）　警備ボックス　トイレ　屋外休憩所　迷子センター　郵便局